The
TRANSFORMING
POWER
of
HEAVEN

**Letting the Presence of God
That's in Heaven Flood into Your Life**

ALLEN MATHER

The Transforming Power of Heaven
Letting the Presence of God That's in Heaven Flood into Your Life
ISBN: 978-1-949106-86-2
Copyright © 2021 by
Allen Mather

You may contact Allen Mather by email:
allenmather1@gmail.com

Published by Word and Spirit Publishing
P.O. Box 701403
Tulsa, Oklahoma 74170
wordandspiritpublishing.com

Cover and Text Design: Lisa Simpson
SimpsonProductions.net

ENDORSEMENT

In *The Transforming Power of Heaven,* Allen Mather has created an invaluable handbook to guide you in your walk with God. Distilling the law, the prophets, and the teachings of Jesus down to the essence of the Christian faith, Mather shows how to experience the presence of God in everyday life.

Whether you are a new believer or a seasoned Christian, *The Transforming Power of Heaven* will keep you close to your love and remind you daily what the Christian life is all about.

Keep this book close to you through the seasons of life. Like a compass, it will keep you on true north in your journey with Jesus.

I have been reading it constantly. It is not a "quick" read. It is a clear and deep resource of inspiration.

Ben Ferrell
President of *BMCFerrell*

DEDICATION

I want to dedicate this book to my wife Ruth. I am so, so thankful to have her. I was an atheist with a lot of problems when we met. She prayed diligently for me year after year. She helped me progress in my relationship with God. She laid down her life for years not only for me and our two sons but hundreds of others. I would not be the person I am today without her. We have had a crazy life together. Thank you Ruth for loving me.

CONTENTS

"The most important aspect of Christianity is not the work we do, but the relationship we maintain (with God) and the surrounding influence and qualities produced by that relationship. That is all God asks us to give our attention to, and it is the one thing that is continually under attack."

Oswald Chambers
My Utmost for His Highest
August 4

When the apostle Paul wrote a letter to the Corinthian church, he was very disturbed by what was happening to them, he wrote this in his letter, "I am jealous for you with the jealousy of God Himself, for I promised you as a pure bride to one husband Christ. But I fear that somehow you will be led away from your pure and simple devotion to Christ." (2 Corinthians 11:2,3 NLT.) Paul was so concerned that they would lose the one thing that was essential, which is pure love and devotion to Christ. I am concerned that in our day of complexity we could lose the one thing we can't afford to lose the one thing we can't live without! I pray this book will inspire us to simplicity and make loving Christ and letting Him love us, be the central focus of our lives.

God's love for us is massive — greater than what we will ever know. This love is what heals us. It gives us purpose, and it gives us peace. This love is what we were made for.

CHAPTER 1

IT'S ALL ABOUT LOVE

To start this book, I want us to start on the right track so as we progress through this book we don't get "off track" by thinking it's about rules or new information apart from the love and companionship of God.

I want this book to be about a deep love relationship with God. There is no other motive in the Bible; that is legitimate! The only motive that God wants is deep love, an all-consuming love for Him. All other motives will lead us astray.

We are the bride of Christ. When two people get married, love must be the only motive – not selfish love, but true love. That is the only motive that will endure. If the motive is money, fame, lust, or pleasure, it won't last. So it is with our relationship with God.

Jesus was very specific about this. When asked by the religious leaders, "What is the greatest commandment?" there was absolutely no hesitation:

"You shall love the Lord your God with all your heart and with all your soul and with all your mind (intellect).

"This is the great (most important, principal) and first commandment.

"And a second is like it: You shall love your neighbor as [you do] yourself.

"These two commandments sum up and upon them depend all the Law and the Prophets."

Matthew 22:37-40

Other translations say the whole Law and the Prophets depend on these two commandments. This is mind-boggling that the entire Bible can be summed up in two Scriptures. This tells us what God really wants and what He is passionate about. That is for us to love Him with all our heart, all our soul, and all our mind.

This is so wonderful that it is all about love – all out love. God does not want anything else from us because He is in love with us. His love is total. He wants love in return.

Jesus said, *"I have loved you, [just] as the Father has loved Me..."* (John 15:9). So here we are locked in love. So how do we move forward? I hope this book will help us move forward and move away from things that don't promote love. All the rules we follow must promote love, first for God and then for man.

As we walk through the Bible, we find something amazing! The God of creation who made everything loves little old me and you! This is hard to grasp, and He loved me even when

I was in sin. He loves us because He is love. This is the main theme of the Bible – that God loves us passionately and desires our companionship. He does not desire rules and regulations apart from what enhances love.

Jesus was very hard on the religious leaders of His day, because it was about outward rules. They did it right on the outside, but Jesus told them they were dead on the inside.

Many people today follow the "Christian" rules, but are dead on the inside. This is why so many young people who grow up in the church leave in their twenties. They did all the rules thinking it would bring life, only to find a deep emptiness.

Many church members are empty deep inside. This is why they look elsewhere for something to give them life, but it's only a temporary fix.

The Bible tells us the greatest possession we can have is to love God. Jesus said in John 5:39-40:

> *"You search and investigate and pore over the Scriptures diligently, because you suppose and trust that you have eternal life through them. And these [very Scriptures] testify about Me!*
>
> *"And still you are not willing [but refuse] to come to Me, so that you might have life."*

So often we think reading our Bible and attending church will bring us life. The Bible only points us to a powerful relationship with God directly. We can read a book on prayer but not pray. We can read the Bible but not come directly to God and pour our hearts out to Him. If we are not careful, our Christian life will be secondhand, hand-me-down Christianity, rather than coming directly to the throne of God.

I don't want this book to just increase your knowledge. I want it to increase your direct intimacy with Christ. As Mother Teresa said, "Jesus and Jesus alone is life." We must speak directly to Him, and let Him speak directly to us – Jesus pouring out His heart to us, and us pouring out our hearts to Him.

The Bible says the greatest of all is love. The Amplified Version of the Bible explains this love. First Corinthians 13:13 says, *"[Love – true affection for God and man, growing out of God's love for and in us]...."* The Bible says this is the greatest of all things. This we must be centered on as we progress through this book. Only the love of Jesus for us, living inside of us, will bring us life.

Jesus said, *"I am the Bread of Life..."* (John 6:48). Taking Jesus into us directly is the only life – Jesus and Jesus alone.

God has a personality. He has desires and a will. In this book, we are going to explore God's great desires and His passionate will. You may feel that part of this book is unattainable. Don't get discouraged. It is God who is in us who will give us the ability.

Some of the words used in this book may seem flowery. That's because our language is so limited, and we are talking about something that is above language; so finding an English word to describe the wonder and amazement of God is difficult, so bear with me. If you find a better word, insert it into the text. Let me know. I hope as you read this book, these are the things you hear. God bless you as you read this book.

I may repeat certain themes as we progress through the book so bear with me. I hope it will help to emphasize certain truths. Some of my sentence structure may not be perfect, please excuse this; I was trying to be true to the original thought. Thank you.

WHAT HAVE WE LEARNED FROM THIS CHAPTER?

The Bible talks about gaining knowledge apart from experiencing God. Most of the Bible is people encountering God, then writing about it. But if we just gain knowledge and don't encounter God, we have missed our whole purpose.

The Bible is a road map to a powerful experience with God. A road map is a tool to get us to a destination. How useless to only study a road map and never let that map lead us to a destination.

Gaining knowledge about God and not letting that knowledge lead us to a powerful relationship with God can be sad and dangerous. My desire is that this book leads us to experience God, not just learn about Him. May the Holy Spirit give you revelation as you read this book.

1. Love is the only legitimate motive. Jesus was clear throughout His ministry that outward acts were not what was pleasing to God, but why you are doing what you are doing. If we are not careful, we will think what

we do is all that counts. Jesus is more concerned with the motive – what is driving you to do what you are doing. Jesus wants our motive for what we are doing to be love for Him – deep love for Him.

2. God's love for us is massive – greater than what we will ever know. This love is what heals us. It gives us purpose, and it gives us peace. This love is what we were made for.

3. Jesus wants to come on the inside of us. He is the Bread of Life. Just as when we eat bread, the chemical energy is diffused throughout every cell, producing energy for our body to move and function. So as we allow Christ to come in, He nourishes every cell of our bodies, bringing divine life and energy with Him.

PRAYER

Holy Spirit, come and make heaven real to me. Illuminate my spirit with Your Spirit. Without You, I cannot see and I cannot feel. Heaven is far away, but You, Holy Spirit, bring heaven to me. You open my eyes and ears to see and hear, so I ask You to come. You are the Promise, the Counselor, the Advocate, and the Illuminator. You are so precious. Thank You for coming and making the invisible visible.

Note: This book is not a to-do list, but a "who to be with" list – to be with the One who loves you, the power-filled only eternal One!

Note: Commands and rules of the Christian life should promote love for God. If what we are doing does not enhance deep love for God, we need to reevaluate what we are doing. Loving Him is the goal. We are in a spiritual marriage and love is the way forward.

THE POWERFUL FORCE IN HEAVEN
THAT MAKES IT ALL WORK IS LOVE.
THE CREATURES IN HEAVEN ARE
TOTALLY IN LOVE WITH GOD, AND
GOD IS TOTALLY IN LOVE WITH THEM.
THIS IS NOT DUTY. THIS IS LOVE.

CHAPTER 2

THE PLACE GOD
HOLDS IN HEAVEN

The words of Christ are so powerful that just a few words from His lips can alter everything.

I want to look at fourteen words that can change the whole direction of our lives with Christ. These fourteen words are found in the Lord's Prayer. We will get to these fourteen words shortly.

The disciples, who for years had observed Jesus' prayer life, had seen Him in all night prayer. They had watched Him pour His heart out to His Father. They saw a powerful, unique, beautiful, and very personal connection with His Father. They observed that connection, but did not know where to start, so they got real bold one day and asked Jesus to teach them how to pray.

We see this recorded in Luke 11:1: *"Then He was praying in a certain place; and when He stopped, one of His disciples said to Him, Lord, teach us to pray, [just] as John taught his disciples."* Jesus, knowing their confusion and desire, taught them how to pray in great detail.

What Jesus taught them is the most important prayer in the Bible. This prayer sets in motion priorities. It tells us what is vitally important. It gives us a pattern to follow, not only for this life, but for all eternity. In this prayer, Jesus was not only sharing His heart with the disciples, but He was giving them amazing direction and priorities. This prayer is short but extremely powerful.

This prayer is found in Luke 11:2 and Matthew 6:9. Let's read the Lord's Prayer from Matthew in the New King James Version.

Our Father in heaven,
Hallowed be Your name.
Your kingdom come.
Your will be done
On earth as it is in heaven.
Give us this day our daily bread.
And forgive us our debts,
As we forgive our debtors.
And do not lead us into temptation,
But deliver us from the evil one.
For Yours is the kingdom and the power and the glory forever.
Amen.

This prayer starts out with addressing God as *"Our Father."* Immediately we are given what type of relationship we have with the God of the universe. He is our Father. We can talk to Him as the One who loves us deeply, cares for us, and watches over us. We are children in His family. We are in a close personal relationship with Him. He hears us, listens to us, gives us His attention, and answers us. He is greater than any earthly father, completely caring and loving.

Jesus talked about how much greater Father God is than any earthly father. We could write a whole book on these two words – "Our Father." This is so deep, so amazing, so wonderful that words cannot express it. A thorough study of these two words, combined with prayer, would be well worth our time.

The next part of the prayer is *"Hallowed be Your name."* This is where we look at God, not ourselves. We gaze at Him like on the Mount of Transfiguration. You will find this encounter with Jesus in Matthew 17:1-9. He becomes separated from all others. He becomes our focus. He is holy and separated. He becomes our life focus, our number one love, separate from all else. This focus puts us in the right perspective to pray. We will see this focus as we look to heaven in this chapter.

We then come to the focus of this book: *"Your kingdom come. Your will be done on earth as it is in heaven."* These are the fourteen words that change everything.

The very first thing Jesus instructs us to pray for is for God's will to be done on earth exactly as it is done in heaven. When we think of the will of God, it can get confusing, so Jesus defines the will of God as that which is going on in heaven. Heaven is the place where the perfect will of God is done. Heaven now becomes our pattern for the will of God and for our Christian life.

Let's take a closer look at heaven. If His will is to be done in my life just like it is in heaven, then what goes on in heaven needs to be our focus and our pattern. Heaven is the center of the universe. Everything comes from this place. This place is the source of everything. Creation, Holy Spirit, God speaks from heaven. All things radiate from this place.

The best glimpses of heaven are found in the book of Revelation. Let's look together at Revelation, chapter 4:

"After this I looked, and behold, a door standing open in heaven! And the first voice which I had heard addressing me like [the calling of] a war trumpet said, Come up here, and I will show you what must take place in the future.

"At once I came under the [Holy] Spirit's power, and behold, a throne stood in heaven, with One seated on the throne!

"And He Who sat there appeared like [the crystalline brightness of] jasper and [the fiery] sardius, and encircling the throne there was a halo that looked like [a rainbow of] emerald.

"Twenty-four other thrones surrounded the throne, and seated on these thrones were twenty-four elders (the members of the heavenly Sanhedrin), arrayed in white clothing, with crowns of gold upon their heads.

"Out from the throne came flashes of lightning and rumblings and peals of thunder, and in front of the throne seven blazing torches burned, which are the seven Spirits of God [the sevenfold Holy Spirit];

"And in front of the throne there was also what looked like a transparent glassy sea, as if of crystal. And around the throne, in the center at each side of the throne, were four living creatures (beings) who were full of eyes in front and behind [with intelligence as to what is before and at the rear of them].

"The first living creature (being) was like a lion, the second living creature like an ox, the third living creature had the face of a man, and the fourth living creature [was] like a flying eagle.

"And the four living creatures, individually having six wings, were full of eyes all over and within [underneath their wings]; and day and night they never stop saying, Holy, holy, holy is the Lord God Almighty (Omnipotent), Who was and Who is and Who is to come.

"And whenever the living creatures offer glory and honor and thanksgiving to Him Who sits on the throne, Who lives forever and ever (through the eternities of the eternities),

"The twenty-four elders (the members of the heavenly Sanhedrin) fall prostrate before Him Who is sitting on the throne, and they worship Him Who lives forever and ever; and they throw down their crowns before the throne, crying out,

"Worthy are You, our Lord and God, to receive the glory and the honor and dominion, for You created all things;

by Your will they were [brought into being] and were created."

It is impossible for words to describe what is going on around the throne of God. Only the Holy Spirit can interpret this intense scene. What is going on here has huge implications for us.

Remember, the first thing we are to ask for in the Lord's Prayer is for *"Your kingdom to come, Your will be done, on earth as it is in heaven."* The kingdom of God is set up in our hearts. Jesus said the kingdom of God is within you, so what we are asking for is that whatever is happening in heaven, we are asking for that to go on in our hearts.

What is going on in heaven? From these verses we see the creatures worshiping God day and night. God is the center of their world. There are no distractions. He is loved with all their hearts, minds, and souls. Because they are in His presence, they can see His beauty and His magnificence. Whenever they offer glory and honor and thanksgiving, they fall prostrate before Him and they worship Him. They throw down their crowns before the throne, crying out, *"Worthy are You ...to receive the glory and the honor and dominion, for You created all things..."* (Revelation 4:11).

If the first thing we are instructed to pray for is God's will to be done in our heart just like it is in heaven, we have a lot of wonderful things to look at and imitate and look forward to. Heaven may look too intense to follow, but if we ask God to help us, draw us to Him, open our spiritual eyes to what is going on in heaven, so heaven can become a reality to us. So let's continue to look at heaven in the next chapter.

Remember, the powerful force in heaven that makes it all work is love. These creatures are totally in love with God, and God is totally in love with them. This is not duty. This is love.

The creatures in heaven don't worship God day and night because they have to. It is a response of seeing God for Who He is.

It is the Holy Spirit who makes this realm real and gives us the ability to live in His universe. John said he was in the presence and power of the Holy Spirit on the Lord's day. His presence is what thrust him into this realm.

Keeping the theme of the first chapter in mind – heaven is held together by love. Worship in heaven is about loving the amazing God with all their hearts.

WHAT HAVE WE LEARNED FROM THIS CHAPTER?

1. As Jesus instructed us in the Lord's Prayer, the first thing we are to pray for is for God's will to be done on earth just as it is in heaven.

2. Heaven now becomes the pattern for God's will in our hearts.

3. Heaven is an intense place because the presence of God is without limit.

4. God is the focus of heaven, and intense worship is the expression of that focus.

5. There is nothing in heaven to distract from devotion to God.

6. What is going on in heaven should be going on in our hearts.

7. Heaven has an exalted view of God. They see Him for who He really is. If we have a low view of God, it will leave us open to a thousand perils.

8. Jesus prayed in John 17:24 that we would see His glory. In heaven they behold His glory.

9. Remember, it is the unlimited presence of God that makes heaven heaven. We so need the presence of God in our lives to make heaven real. Heaven is Holy Spirit dependent.

Note: John saw a door standing open in heaven. That door is open to us today just like it was for John. The Holy Spirit will help us walk through this door.

Note: Remember, this is not to happen by our own strength or intellect; it is the Holy Spirit that will accomplish this in us. We need to <u>ask</u> for His presence. We need to be Holy Spirit dependent. We become more aware of the Holy Spirit by asking God to make Himself real to us. See Luke 11:13.

PRAYER

God, I ask You to make heaven real to me. I need to feel heaven in my heart. I need to sense the reality of heaven. Your realm is the real realm, the beautiful realm, the perfect realm. God, I want it to dominate my heart.

Note: John, before he saw heaven, said, "At once I came under the Holy Spirit's power. What we will be discussing in this book can only be comprehended by the power of the Holy Spirit. Jesus sent the Holy Spirit to us to interpret these amazing things. Only the Holy Spirit can interpret these things. The human intellect cannot. So as we progress through this book, continue to ask the Holy Spirit to make these things alive and real.

Remember, this book is not about rules. It's about a love relationship with a God who loves us massively and wants us to talk with Him, spend time with Him, just wants us to love Him back, that's all. Then all the changes we desire come from that love. When the motive is intense love, great things can happen.

MANY PEOPLE ARE TRYING TO
FIGURE OUT WHAT THE CHRISTIAN
LIFE SHOULD LOOK LIKE. IN THE
LORD'S PRAYER, JESUS IS LETTING US
KNOW IT SHOULD LOOK LIKE HEAVEN.

CHAPTER 3

THE PLACE JESUS HOLDS IN HEAVEN

In the previous chapter, we looked at what goes on in heaven from the book of Revelation. In the Lord's Prayer, the prayer Jesus gave us, the first thing we are to ask for is for the kingdom of God to come into our hearts just like it is in heaven.

Many people are trying to figure out what the Christian life should look like. Here in the Lord's Prayer, Jesus is letting us know it should <u>look like heaven</u>. So let's look at some more things that go on in heaven.

In chapter 5 in the book of Revelation, there is an amazing event that takes place. This event reveals the place Jesus holds in heaven. Let's read chapter 5 together, thinking of the Lord's Prayer: Your will be done in my heart as it is in heaven. Our prayer is, Holy Spirit, we want the place Jesus holds in heaven to be the place He holds in my heart.

> *"And I saw lying on the open hand of Him Who was seated on the throne a scroll (book) written within and on the back, closed and sealed with seven seals;*
>
> *"And I saw a strong angel announcing in a loud voice, Who is worthy to open the scroll? And [who is entitled and deserves and is morally fit] to break its seals?*
>
> *"And no one in heaven or on earth or under the earth [in the realm of the dead, Hades] was able to open the scroll or to take a [single] look at its contents.*
>
> *"And I wept audibly and bitterly because no one was found fit to open the scroll or to inspect it.*
>
> *"Then one of the elders [of the heavenly Sanhedrin] said to me, Stop weeping! See, the Lion of the tribe of Judah, the Root (Source) of David, has won (has overcome and conquered)! He can open the scroll and break its seven seals!*
>
> *"And there between the throne and the four living creatures (beings) and among the elders [of the heavenly Sanhedrin] I saw a Lamb standing, as though it had been slain, with seven horns and with seven eyes, which are the seven Spirits of God [the sevenfold Holy Spirit] Who have been sent [on duty far and wide] into all the earth.*
>
> *"He then went and took the scroll from the right hand of Him Who sat on the throne.*
>
> *"And when He had taken the scroll, the four living creatures and the twenty-four elders [of the heavenly Sanhedrin] prostrated themselves before the Lamb. Each was holding*

a harp (lute or guitar), and they had golden bowls full of incense (fragrant spices and gums for burning), which are the prayers of God's people (the saints).

"And [now] they sing a new song, saying, You are worthy to take the scroll and to break the seals that are on it, for You were slain (sacrificed), and with Your blood You purchased men unto God from every tribe and language and people and nation.

"And You have made them a kingdom (royal race) and priests to our God, and they shall reign [as kings] over the earth!

"Then I looked, and I heard the voices of many angels on every side of the throne and of the living creatures and the elders [of the heavenly Sanhedrin], and they numbered ten thousand times ten thousand and thousands of thousands,

"Saying in a loud voice, Deserving is the Lamb, Who was sacrificed, to receive all the power and riches and wisdom and might and honor and majesty (glory, splendor) and blessing!

"And I heard every created thing in heaven and on earth and under the earth [in Hades, the place of departed spirits] and on the sea and all that is in it, crying out together, To Him Who is seated on the throne and to the Lamb be ascribed the blessing and the honor and the majesty (glory, splendor) and the power (might and dominion) forever and ever (through the eternities of the eternities)!

"Then the four living creatures (beings) said, Amen (so be it)! And the elders [of the heavenly Sanhedrin] prostrated

themselves and worshiped Him Who lives forever and ever.

Revelation 5:1-14

What we see in this chapter is the place Jesus holds in heaven. In heaven, Jesus is deeply worshiped as the Lamb Who was slain for us. He is seen as the only One worthy to take the scroll. When He does, the elders and the living creatures fall face down and worship Him.

New songs of praise are sung to the Lamb, describing what He has done, how worthy He is, how He paid the price for our redemption, purchasing us to bring us to God. He chose us to serve God and formed us into a kingdom of priests who reign on earth. Let's look at this again.

"Then I looked, and I heard the voices of many angels on every side of the throne and of the living creatures and the elders [of the heavenly Sanhedrin], and they numbered ten thousand times ten thousand and thousands of thousands,

"Saying in a loud voice, Deserving is the Lamb, Who was sacrificed, to receive all the power and riches and wisdom and might and honor and majesty (glory, splendor) and blessing!

"And I heard every created thing in heaven and on earth and under the earth [in Hades, the place of departed spirits] and on the sea and all that is in it, crying out together, To Him Who is seated on the throne and to the Lamb be ascribed the blessing and the honor and the majesty (glory, splendor) and the power (might and dominion) forever and ever (through the eternities of the eternities)!

"Then the four living creatures (beings) said, Amen (so be it)! And the elders [of the heavenly Sanhedrin] prostrated themselves and worshiped Him Who lives forever and ever."

What was just read is almost incomprehensible. The place Jesus holds in heaven is indescribable – a place that is incomprehensible to the natural mind. It's like trying to comprehend the universe. But what we see is He holds a place like no other, and as it said before in the Lord's Prayer, "Your kingdom come on earth as it is in heaven." Jesus is to take this exact place in our hearts that He holds in heaven: loved and adored above all other things.

God, we ask You to show this to us, work this into us, give us heaven's single eye. May we turn our eyes upon Jesus as He is adored in heaven. May we adore Him in our hearts as He is adored in heaven.

WHAT HAVE WE LEARNED FROM THIS CHAPTER?

1. Jesus was the only One in all of heaven Who was worthy to open the scroll and break the seals.

2. Jesus is the Lamb Who was slain for us, to bring us to God.

3. When Jesus took the scroll from the Father, the heavenly Sanhedrin prostrated themselves before the Lamb.

4. The Sanhedrin was holding golden bowls full of incense, which are the prayers of God's people.

5. They sang a new song, saying, "You are worthy to take the scroll and break the seals...with Your blood You purchased men for God" (v. 9).

6. Jesus has made us a kingdom (royal race) and priests to God. That means we have direct access to God. We can go to the throne room of God; we are welcome there.

7. There were many voices of angels and living creatures and elders, ten thousand times ten thousand and thousands of thousands saying in a loud voice, *"Deserving is the Lamb, Who was sacrificed, to receive all the power and riches and wisdom and might and honor and majesty (glory, splendor) and blessing!"* (v. 12).

8. He heard every created thing in heaven and on earth and under the earth, on the sea, and all that is in it, crying out together to God and the Lamb, be ascribed blessing and honor and majesty (glory, splendor) and power (might and dominion) forever and ever. Then the four living creatures said, "Amen," and the elders prostrated themselves and worshiped Him who lives forever (vv. 13-14).

9. What we just read is what needs to take place in us. The place Jesus holds in heaven is the place He should hold in our hearts. The Holy Spirit wants to make this possible.

---

10. Remember, this is about love. The creatures in heaven love Jesus with everything in them. It's not about duty. It's spontaneous love.

11. The unlimited presence of the Holy Spirit makes this possible. This is why we desperately need the strong presence of the Holy Spirit.

12. Let's ask for the Holy Spirit. We can't even see the kingdom of God without the presence of the Holy Spirit (Read John 3:3).

13. Look at the teaching in Luke 11:13: *"If you then, evil as you are, know how to give good gifts [gifts that are to their advantage] to your children, how much more will your heavenly Father give the Holy Spirit to those who ask and continue to ask Him!"* We don't work to receive the Holy Spirit — we simply ask. He is a free gift.

14. We desperately need the Holy Spirit to see Jesus high and lifted up.

PRAYER

God, we are desperate for the reality of Your Holy Spirit in our lives. Without Your active Spirit, we can't even see the heavenly realm. Make my spirit alive to You so that I may see how incredibly wonderful You are and love You back with all of my heart.

JOHN, IN THE BOOK OF REVELATION, SAID, *"I WAS IN THE SPIRIT [RAPT IN HIS POWER] ON THE LORD'S DAY, AND I HEARD BEHIND ME A GREAT VOICE..."* (REVELATION 1:10). IT WAS THE HOLY SPIRIT WHO REVEALED THESE THINGS TO JOHN. THIS IS WHY WE <u>MUST</u> ASK THE SPIRIT TO SHOW THESE MARVELOUS THINGS TO US AND HELP US APPLY THEM TO OUR LIVES.

CHAPTER 4

A VOICE FROM HEAVEN
(GOD'S NUMBER ONE DESIRE)

I n the last chapter, we looked at the place Jesus holds in heaven. There are no earthly words to describe that place. There are songs in heaven about Him, decrees in heaven about Him, angels lying prostrate before Him, beings in heaven worshiping Him. These things can only be interpreted by the Holy Spirit. One thing can be said. He holds a central place like no other.

Remember, John in the book of Revelation said, *"I was in the Spirit [rapt in His power] on the Lord's Day, and I heard behind me a great voice..."* (1:10). It was the Holy Spirit who revealed these things to John. This is why we must ask the Spirit to show these marvelous things to us and help us apply them to our lives.

There is another event in heaven that has huge implications for us. In Revelation 21:3 there is a *mighty voice* from the throne of God. John said, this is a mighty voice. So as you read it, read with a loud voice. *"I perceived its distinct words...."* The words were, *"See! The abode of God is with men, and He will live (encamp, tent) among them; and they shall be His people, and God shall personally be with them and be their God."*

This proclamation is the whole theme of the Bible. Over fifty times from Genesis to Revelation, God declares His great desire that He wants to live with us and for us to be His people.

At the end of the chapter, I will list many of these Scriptures. This is God's greatest desire. Jesus declares this on the great day of the feast. Jesus stood and He cried in a loud voice, *"If any man is thirsty, let him come to Me and drink!"* (John 7:37). Jesus prayed in John 17:24, *"Father, I desire that they also whom You have entrusted to Me [as Your gift to Me] may be with Me where I am, so that they may see My glory...."* God wants where we dwell to be His dwelling place. No separate dwellings. One dwelling place together.

Paul said in 1 Corinthians 6:17, *"But the person who is united to the Lord becomes one spirit with Him."* He wants to dwell inside our spirit and we become one with Him.

In Revelation 3:20 Jesus says, *"Behold, I stand at the door and knock; if anyone hears and listens to and heeds My voice and opens the door, I will come in to him and will eat with him, and he [will eat] with Me."* This indicates deep fellowship.

Jesus said in John 17:23, *"I in them and You in Me, in order that they may become one and perfectly united...."* That's how close He wants to be to us. Jesus in me and I in Him.

This *booming voice* from heaven is not a timid voice or a quiet voice. This is the overwhelming desire of God, trying to let a sleeping humanity know His passionate desire. THE DWELLING PLACE OF GOD IS WITH MEN, OR THE DWELLING PLACE OF GOD IS INSIDE MANKIND. You are the temple of the Holy Spirit (1 Corinthians 6:19), and God wants to live inside you.

WHAT HAVE WE LEARNED FROM THIS CHAPTER?

1. In Revelation 21:3, there was a mighty voice coming from the throne of God. The words were: *"See! The abode of God is with men, and He will live (encamp, tent) among them; and they shall be His people, and God shall personally be with them and be their God."*

2. This proclamation came from the throne of God. This is the cry of God's heart. This cry is the theme of the whole Bible.

3. God wants to live with us and live in us (Read 1 Corinthians 6:17, Revelation 3:20, John 7:37).

4. Jesus in His last prayer before He was betrayed in John 17:24 said, *"Father, I desire that they also whom You have entrusted to Me [as Your gift to Me] may be with Me where I am, so that they may see My glory...."* This is the number one desire of God: companionship with us. This is to be the main direction of our lives.

The dwelling place of God is among men as each of the following Scriptures reveal. This is the theme of the whole Bible. This is God's passionate desire, His overwhelming passion, to dwell inside us. We have become His temple where He desires to live. This is where we need to put our attention:

Revelation 21:3
2 Corinthians 6:16
Exodus 29:4-5
Jeremiah 32:38
Hebrews 8:10
Leviticus 26:12
Ezekiel 37:26-27
Ezekiel 11:20
Jeremiah 31:33
Zechariah 2:10-11
Hosea 2:23
1 Corinthians 3:16-17
Jeremiah 24:7
Revelation 21:7
Zechariah 8:8
1 Corinthians 6:19
Zechariah 13:9
Romans 8:11
1 John 4:15
Ezekiel 36:28
Genesis 17:7-8
Ephesians 3:17
1 John 5:20-21
John 6:56
Hebrews 3:6

1 Peter 2:5
Romans 9:26
1 John 4:12
2 Timothy 1:14
Ezekiel 43:9
Ezekiel 43:7
Joshua 24:14-24
Exodus 34:14
Romans 8:9
Exodus 23:13
Ephesians 2:20
Matthew 6:24
Psalm 90:1
1 Samuel 7:3-4
Deuteronomy 4:23-24
Exodus 20:3
Ezekiel 36:25
2 Chronicles 33:4-5
Deuteronomy 6:14-15
Revelation 2:1

PRAYER

Father, Your great desire, the number one desire of Your heart, is to dwell in us and for us to dwell in You. I ask You to change my heart to where this is my number one desire: to dwell in You and to allow you to dwell in me. I want my heart to be your home, your resting place.

Psalm 73:25 states, *"Whom have I in heaven but You? And I have no delight or desire on earth besides You."* The psalmist made a great declaration so clear, so insightful, and so precise. "I have no one but You in heaven," or to simplify it, "I have no one but You."

CHAPTER 5

I HAVE NO ONE
BUT YOU IN HEAVEN

"Whom have I in heaven but You? And I have no delight or desire on earth besides You."

Psalm 73:25

The Psalmist made a great declaration so clear, so insightful, and so precise. "I have no one but You in heaven," or to simplify it, "I have no one but You."

We live in a temporal world, and life is so short. Everything we have and all we have worked for will be taken from us at death because all we see, taste, touch, smell, and feel are not permanent. Knowing this makes our choices so much easier. I can pursue temporal things that can be taken from me any second, or I can pursue eternal things that will never be taken from me for all eternity. It's what we call a no-brainer.

Jesus talked a lot about the temporal and the eternal. In John 6:27 Jesus says, *"Stop toiling and doing and producing for the food that perishes and decomposes [in the using], but strive and work and produce rather for the [lasting] food which endures [continually] unto life eternal...."*

"Don't be so concerned about perishable things like food. Spend your energy seeking the eternal life that the Son of Man can give you. For God the Father has given me the seal of his approval" (John 6:27 NLT).

Here Jesus is contrasting the eternal with the temporal. The value of the temporal is so much less than the eternal. In many ways, I am glad I live in a temporal world. This world is dying. It makes seeking the eternal the only logical choice.

Modern science is verifying that all is temporal. The cosmological forecast (the fate of the universe) is grim. Our sun one day will use up all its hydrogen and will become a white dwarf, burning up the earth and all the planets. At some point, all of the stars in the universe will "burn" through all their hydrogen; stars will die one at a time, leaving a dark, cold universe where no life exists — just cold blackness. Even our earth and universe have no future apart from God. So we are left with only the logical choice: ***Seek the eternal!***

In the verse we just read from John 6:27, Jesus says to spend your energy seeking the eternal life that the Son of Man can give you.

So we ask, "What is the eternal life that we should seek?" Jesus clears this up in John 17:3: *"And this is eternal life: [it means] to know (to perceive, recognize, become acquainted with, and understand) You, the only true and real God, and [likewise] to know Him, Jesus [as the] Christ (the Anointed One, the Messiah), Whom You have sent."*

The Greek word for "to know" or "to take in knowledge" is *ginosko*. It is not intellectual knowledge, but by operation of the Holy Spirit. It is an infusing of who God is into us where He becomes a part of our DNA or our body. This is why Jesus told the disciples to eat of His flesh and drink of His blood. Very offensive in the natural, but Jesus was speaking of His divine life entering into us to where we are part of Him and He is part of us. This is the essence of eternal life. Read John 6:56.

Jesus says in John 17:23, *"I in them and You in Me...."* This is an amazing reality. Jesus coming into us, giving us His life, which changes us into new beings. We are now able to develop a real relationship with Him. We can know Him, hear His voice, feel His presence, see Him with our spiritual eyes, feel His love, talk directly to Him, and know that He hears us. This is what eternal life with Jesus is.

In John 3:3, Jesus said to Nicodemus "I assure you, most solemnly I tell you, that unless a person is born again (anew, from above), he cannot see (know, be acquainted with, and experience) the kingdom of God." When you are born the first time from your mother's womb you were introduced to a fascinating world. You heard your mother and father's voices, you saw light, you were hungry, you felt touch, and pain. You ended up in an amazing realm. Jesus said there is another realm, the realm of the spirit that you can be born into. Just like your first birth, this second birth thrusts you into another realm of sound and sight, a reality beyond this reality, a reality of the eternal. And we are welcome there.

Because of this miracle, we are able to enter into the heavenly realm — see and hear things coming from the eternal world. Heaven becomes real and becomes our focus, and we are transformed. It is wonderful that in reality we have only Jesus; all else will fail us. It makes our choices simple. So instead of material things being our focus, taking all of our energy, knowing Jesus can now be the focus of our energy – our life's pursuit.

WHAT HAVE WE LEARNED FROM THIS CHAPTER?

1. In heaven and earth we have no one but Jesus (Psalm 73:25).

2. Everything we see, taste, touch, smell, and feel is temporal and will dissolve to nothing in the end (2 Corinthians 4:18, Hebrews 13:14).

3. Jesus said in John 6:27, *"Stop toiling and doing and producing for the food that perishes and decomposes [in the using], but STRIVE and WORK and PRODUCE rather for the [lasting] food which endures [continually] unto life eternal...."*

4. Jesus defined "eternal life" as to know Him intimately, to converse with Him, for Him to become our companion (John 17:23).

5. We need a larger world view. One that looks hundreds of years into the future. One that will make sense in 1000 years.

PRAYER

God, come and reveal these marvelous things to my heart. Take away the distractions that make me focus on lesser things. I want You as my primary focus, because I know that everything except You is decomposing around me. In the end, Your love for me is the only thing that will endure. Thank You for letting me see this amazing truth.

According to Jesus, heaven is not just a future event, but it is also a present reality. If we are to pray for His kingdom to come now as it is in heaven, then the kingdom we are praying for is not just a future event. We are to ask for it now.

CHAPTER 6

INTERACTING WITH HEAVEN

We have been looking at the Lord's Prayer. In this prayer, the first thing we are to pray for is for His kingdom to come to earth as it is in heaven. So Jesus is saying that heaven is to be the pattern for the Christian life. No other pattern is given but heaven, so let's continue to explore heaven. (The kingdom of God and heaven are the same. Heaven is the kingdom of God.) Jesus had a lot to say about the kingdom of heaven.

According to Jesus, heaven is not just a future event, but it is also a present reality. If we are to pray for His kingdom to come now as it is in heaven, then the kingdom we are praying for is not just a future event. We are to ask for it now.

There are things coming to us from heaven, and we are sending things up to heaven. Heaven is closer to us than we realize. In Ephesians 2:6 Paul says, *"And He raised us up together with Him and made us sit down together [giving us joint seating with Him] in the heavenly sphere....* "Because we are now seated in the heavenly realm, interaction with heaven is not just a future event but a present reality.

Jesus interacted with heaven His whole ministry. When He was baptized, a voice came from heaven. Matthew 3:16-17 says:

> *"And when Jesus was baptized, He went up at once out of the water; and behold, the heavens were opened, and he [John] saw the Spirit of God descending like a dove and alighting on Him.*
>
> *"And behold, a voice from heaven said, This is My Son, My Beloved, in Whom I delight!"*

This was the start of Jesus' earthly ministry, and the Father was giving Him words of affirmation because He was going to face much temptation and opposition.

We need to realize that God from heaven is speaking these same words to us: "You are My much loved son or daughter, in whom I delight." We will need these words of affirmation ourselves to face the difficulties ahead. We need to know that God delights in us and enjoys our friendship. Jesus says, "I no longer call you servants but friends." (See John 15:15.)

Jesus was constantly interacting with heaven. In John 5:19 Jesus said, *"I assure you, most solemnly I tell you, the Son is able to do nothing of Himself (of His own accord); but He is able to do only what He sees the Father doing...."* His eyes were glued to heaven.

Jesus was constantly communicating with His Father in heaven. The heavenly encounters in Jesus' life were too many to mention in this chapter. His life on earth began when an angel from heaven declared to Mary, *"And listen! You will become pregnant and will give birth to a Son, and you shall call His name Jesus"* (Luke 1:31).

Jesus' ministry ended on earth in Luke 24:51: *"And it occurred that while He was blessing them, He parted from them and was taken up into heaven."*

The whole life of Jesus from the beginning of His earthly life to the end was an intense interaction with heaven.

The early Christians and the apostles were constantly interacting with heaven. Paul talks about interacting with heaven in 2 Corinthians 12:2-4. He called it the third heaven. The third heaven is the realm where God dwells and the presence of God is without limit. Paul said he heard utterances beyond the power of man to put into words, which man is not permitted to utter. Paul was constantly interacting with heaven, but on this occasion it became so much clearer.

When Stephen was stoned, in Acts 7:55-56 it says:

"But he, full of the Holy Spirit and controlled by Him, gazed into heaven and saw the glory (the splendor and majesty) of God, and Jesus standing at God's right hand;

"And he said, Look! I see the heavens opened, and the Son of man standing at God's right hand!"

Stephen was interacting with heaven.

John, on the Island of Patmos said, *"I was in the Spirit [rapt in His power] on the Lord's Day, and I heard behind me a great voice like the calling of a war trumpet"* (Revelation 1:10). And so began the incredible book of Revelation. These interactions are so many that they would fill a whole book, from Paul meeting Jesus on the Damascus road to Peter on a roof to pray. *"And he saw the sky opened and something like a great sheet lowered by the four corners, descending to the earth"* (Acts 10:11).

I am sure you could find hundreds of these encounters as you read through the Bible. The veil was torn in the temple when Jesus was crucified, making a way for us to enter into the place where God dwells. The connection we have with God, Jesus, and the heavenly realm is astonishing. This is not to be the abnormal but the normal.

There is nothing on God's end preventing us from entering the realm where He lives. We don't seek supernatural experiences, but we do seek Him, and He is supernatural.

The greatest way we interact with heaven is through the Holy Spirit. First Peter 1:12 says, *"[It is these very] things which have now already been made known plainly to you by those who preached the good news (the Gospel) to you by the [same] Holy Spirit sent from heaven...."*

It is so wonderful that even angels are eagerly watching these things happen. The Holy Spirit who lives inside of us comes to us from heaven. The Holy Spirit has the substance of heaven. The Holy Spirit makes heaven real to us. Jesus said the Holy Spirit would take what is His and reveal it to us. (John

16:14.) The Holy Spirit enables us to interact with God in heaven. This is a marvelous thing.

Colossians 3:1-3 says:

"If then you have been raised with Christ [to a new life, thus sharing His resurrection from the dead], aim at and seek the [rich, eternal treasures] that are above, where Christ is, seated at the right hand of God.

"And set your minds and keep them set on what is above (the higher things), not on the things that are on the earth.

"For [as far as this world is concerned] you have died, and your [new, real] life is hidden with Christ in God."

These verses give us tremendous direction for our lives to aim at and seek the rich, eternal treasures that are above, where Christ is seated at the right hand of God. Set your minds and keep them set on what is above. This is such a clear direction for life. It is the only direction that makes sense. It is very countercultural; it goes against all we hear in our world around us. But it's time we go in the opposite direction, because Jesus went in the opposite direction. It's so wonderful to have a different direction – one full of God and full of eternal life.

Don't be conformed to the world around you, but be transformed. (Romans 12:2). What God is offering us is Himself. In us, through us, penetrating every cell of our being – a union so powerful it can't be put into words. It is above anything we could dream of or think of.

This realm is so above this earthly realm, it is staggering. Let's go there. Ask God to take you there. This is His number one desire that we be with Him where He is.

WHAT HAVE WE LEARNED FROM THIS CHAPTER?

1. Heaven is not just a future event, but heaven is in our midst. The Holy Spirit makes us able to interact with heaven (Colossians 3:1-3).

2. We are citizens of heaven now, not just in the future. As citizens, we interact with heaven on a moment by moment basis (Philippians 3:20, Ephesians 2:19, Colossians 3:1).

3. Jesus interacted with heaven (John 5:19).

4. Paul interacted with heaven (Acts 9:3-6).

5. Stephen interacted with heaven (Acts 7:56).

6. John interacted with heaven (Revelation 1:10).

7. Early Christians interacted with heaven (Acts 2).

8. Peter interacted with heaven (Acts 10:11).

9. The way we interact with heaven is through the Holy Spirit (1 Peter 1:12).

10. The Holy Spirit makes it possible to have conversations with the Father, the Son, and Himself. We can go to the throne room of God and pour out our hearts to Him.

PRAYER

Father, thank You that by sending the Holy Spirit, it is now possible to interact with You in heaven. Thank You for giving us the Holy Spirit now when we so desperately need Him. Thank You for Your intense love that flows to us from heaven. Thank You for the union we have with You.

History is filled with times where heaven came to earth and filled a location. The results are so amazing, so supernatural, it's even hard to describe because it is a different substance, and most people are not familiar with it. In heaven it is described as light and glory.

CHAPTER 7

THE ASBURY REVIVAL

In the previous chapters, we talked about the main ingredient in heaven is the presence of God. This presence is not just a proximity to, but it permeates everything. It goes through everything in heaven, changing everything in heaven. This is why heaven is so different. We are to pray for that presence to come to earth and transform us here. *Thy kingdom come on earth as it is in heaven.* (See Matthew 6:10.)

History is filled with times where heaven came to earth and filled a location. The results are so amazing, so supernatural, it's even hard to describe because it is a different substance, and most are not familiar with it. In heaven it is described as light and glory.

When I was in college, I was attending a college called Asbury College. It is now Asbury University. I was pursuing a philosophy and religion degree. I was aware that in the past there were some very amazing times when God's Spirit would descend on the school. It was an independent college but had Methodist roots. We had chapel three times a week for one hour. We mostly sang hymns and heard speakers. It was during the seventies.

There was a lot of unrest, protest, and anger, and buildings were being burned down across our country – a time of great protest and unrest.

Many students on our campus were moderately interested in God, but many were not interested at all. Their parents made them attend. There was a small group who thought things could change through prayer. They began to pray for God's kingdom to come to earth as it is in heaven. They started with seven students; then each seven got seven students. Before long, there was a significant number praying.

I was living off campus, so I was not involved with the praying, but I could tell something was happening. It came to a head one night in February when they all met in the chapel for all-night prayer. They had become desperate for God's presence to come. They became gripped with the desires of heaven.

About 3:00 in the morning, God said, "You have it. It will come to pass." They went to their dorms and went to sleep.

The next morning was chapel. The dean was supposed to speak. Instead, he let the students share. One student, who had been at the prayer meeting the night before, got up and began to speak. God's presence was radiating from him, and it was so strong it immediately changed the atmosphere of the meeting.

We had a large altar rail that extended across the entire front. Students started coming forward to pray and get things right in their lives. Then they would get up and share what God had shown them. The presence of God got stronger and stronger, so they canceled classes. It continued all day and all night for 185 hours. People would sit in the chapel for hours on end. It was like there was no time. Hours felt like minutes. No one got bored. We just wanted to be where God was. Nothing else mattered. God was all there was. He was the central figure, and we wanted to worship Him day and night.

God's presence had come upon us. News media picked it up, and colleges and churches wanted us to come and share about what had happened. We began to travel to churches, colleges, and high schools. Everywhere we went the same thing that had happened to us happened to them. The powerful presence of God came down.

We would get up and share what God had done in us, and it was like a bomb went off. People would run to the front weeping and praying.

What happened at Asbury completely changed the way I viewed Christianity and the church. I saw the great desire God had to be with His people, for there was to be no separation between heaven and earth. The veil had been torn in two, and God was coming to His people (Matthew 27:51).

What happened at my college defies explanation – how a college in 1970 filled with students who could care less about God suddenly made God the central figure of their lives and attended a chapel meeting voluntarily for 185 hours, day and night.

The excitement, the wonder, and the awe these students felt can only be explained by a supernatural force that descended upon them. This happened to the early church in the upper room. Luke describes this encounter in Acts 2:2: *"When suddenly there came a sound from heaven like the rushing of a violent tempest blast, and it filled the whole house in which they were sitting."*

This is the only explanation as to what happened to us at Asbury College. It completely changed my life. I then began to understand God's power in a new way.

During the revival, an older lady got up to speak from the platform and said, "You all are ruined." We were like, "What do you mean?" She said, "Once you have seen God move, you will never be satisfied with the efforts of men again."

Yes, we did get ruined. We saw something that God could do beyond programs, beyond the strategies of men. We saw into the power of the church in the book of Acts.

I am so grateful I got to see and experience this early in my Christian life. It has been a bright beacon to my soul, pointing me to prayer, the presence of God, and keeping my mind on heaven.

History is full of times when God's presence descends to earth like a microburst from heaven. In 1801, Daniel Boone invited a man named Barton Stone to hold a service in Kentucky. It was to be a four-day extended observance of the Lord's Supper. Twenty thousand people came expecting a blessing from God. What happened was completely unexpected – something so supernatural it defied reason.

The realm of heaven invaded the earth. A man named James B. Finley, who later became a Methodist circuit rider, gave an eyewitness account of what happened.

"The noise was like the roar of Niagara. The vast sea of human beings seemed to be agitated as if by a storm.

"I counted seven ministers all preaching at one time, some on stumps, others in wagons, and one standing on a tree, which had fallen, lodged against another. Some of the people were singing, others praying, some crying for mercy in the most piteous accents, while others were shouting vociferously.

"While witnessing these scenes, a peculiarly strange sensation, such as I had never felt, came over me. My heart beat tumultuously, my knees trembled, my lips quivered, and I felt as though I must fall to the ground. A strange supernatural power seemed to pervade the entire mass of mind collected...

"I stepped up on a log where I could have a better view of the surging sea of humanity. The scene that then presented itself to my mind was indescribable. At one time I saw at least five hundred swept down in a moment as if a battery of a thousand guns had been opened upon them, and then immediately followed shrieks and shouts that rent the very heaven."[1]

The Methodist and Baptist took this revival and spread it throughout the frontier. These events defy any natural explanation.

---

[1] Dr. Mendell Taylor. *Exploring Evangelism,* 142.

My experience with the Asbury Revival[2] showed me that these things are supernatural and are sent from heaven.

A revival broke out in Philadelphia under the preaching of George Whitfield in 1744. Benjamin Franklin described the results: "It was wonderful to see the change soon made in the manners of our inhabitants — from being thoughtless or indifferent about religion. It seemed as if all the world were growing religious so that one could not walk through the town in an evening without hearing Psalms sung in different families of every street." Even Benjamin Franklin was puzzled by what happened in Philadelphia.

The history of revivals or awakenings is a fascinating study of what happens when heaven comes to earth. It is so mysterious, so fascinating, so other worldly that study on your own will change your perspective of what God likes to do. "His will be done on earth as in heaven."

America and England have had astonishing times when heaven came to earth. These were described as awakenings. From 1740 to 1750, the first great awakening swept through England and the thirteen colonies in America. Preachers like George Whitfield and Jonathan Edwards helped to spread the awakening.

The second great awakening spread through New England with Charles Finney and through the south and west with camp meetings similar to Cane Ridge. We don't have the time in this book to explore these awakenings further. A study on your own would be very beneficial.

---

[2] Source for Asbury Revival: *When God Comes,* Documentary about the 1970 Revival, YouTube.

WHAT HAVE WE LEARNED FROM THIS CHAPTER?

1. Heaven (God's presence) can come to earth in an astonishing way.

2. When we ask for His kingdom to come to earth like heaven, history tells us amazing things can happen.

3. It is God's will for His presence to come to earth as it is in heaven transforming us.

PRAYER

Thank You, God, that Your number one desire is to bring heaven to us. We ask You to open up heaven to us, and pour its contents into us. We are so aware that we need You. We need Your presence more than life itself. Put within our hearts an intense desire for heaven to descend upon us, our families, and our nations.

Sources for the Asbury Revival on YouTube:
The Asbury Revival 1970
The story of the Asbury College Revival
The 1970 Asbury College Revival - Documentary
Asbury College Revival 1970 (Full)
Deeper Still: Memories of God's Power and Love in the 1970...
A Revival Account: Asbury 1970
"When God Comes" Documentary about the 1970...

Heaven is speaking to us today with encouragement and correction. The word at the end of each letter in the book of Revelation is, *"Listen to what the Spirit has to say to the church."* So in our day, we must listen to what the Spirit is saying to us. He has personal words for each individual and each church. Sometimes it comes as correction, but that is good. That is how we stay in God's plan.

CHAPTER 8

A LIFE OF WORSHIP

One of the main features in heaven is worship. Worship is the result of God's presence. It is not an intellectual decision, but a response to the overwhelming presence of God.

When I was in college and the Holy Spirit fell on us at chapel, one of the main things that happened was worship. We could not refrain from worship. We worshiped and prayed day and night. This was the only response we could give as the presence of God entered the room.

As I have said before, the Christian life is a response to the Holy Spirit's presence. I grew up as an atheist. No amount of argument would have changed my mind. My mind was made up.

I started to date a girl who later became my wife. We met under very unusual circumstances. She told me she would go out with me if I would meet her father. When I showed up at the house, her father looked at her mother privately and said, "That is the person she will marry. I dreamed of him two years ago." Her mom said, "Don't tell her. I don't want her to marry someone because of a dream."

Her father was a very devout follower of Christ, and he wasn't freaked out that his daughter was dating an atheist. He just began praying.

After a while, I started to feel a weird sensation that was making me think about Jesus. It was something I had never felt before. I knew it was not just an emotion, because I had never felt it before. It kept getting stronger, and it really started to mess with me.

I started to go to a little church with her parents. When the pastor would preach, I would feel that presence very strong. I would kind of hang on to the chair and think, "This will be over soon."

One Sunday, the pastor gave an invitation to receive Christ. I went forward and knelt down. The pastor asked if I would like to invite Jesus to come into my heart. I said, "Yes." He asked me to pray. I asked Jesus to come into my life, and to my shock, I felt Him come in.

He asked me if I wanted to pray and I said yes. I started to pray and could not stop. I prayed about things I had never thought of. I just kept going. It was like a dam opened up and God's presence flooded in. He let me keep on praying and did not dismiss church until I was done. I am sure a lot of people were wondering when I was going to finish. Then I heard God's voice. He told me He wanted me to be a missionary. That freaked everyone out because I was planning on being an architect.

I was totally overwhelmed. I did not think it would last because I had a lot of things to overcome, but Jesus stuck with me and helped me overcome all kinds of problems, and He became a powerful force in my life.

The reason for telling this is that the things that happen spiritually to us are a response to the Holy Spirit. He initiates by His presence, and we respond. This is what makes true worship possible. It is a response to the presence of God.

I have been in meetings where God's presence came and people worshiped for five or six hours, and it seemed like minutes. This is why heaven is so different. When God's presence is there without measure, remarkable things happen. The creatures don't worship God all day and night on their own. It is a response to an overwhelming presence. So it is with us in true heart worship and prayer. These things are a result of the force of God coming upon us. Like the force of gravity shapes our universe, the force of the Holy Spirit shapes our spiritual life. This is what powered the New Testament church.

The book of Acts was not the acts of the apostles as some say, but the acts of the Holy Spirit. The new believers responded to this new force or power that had come upon them. Jesus told these new believers, "And now I will send the Holy Spirit, just as My Father promised. But stay here in the city until the Holy Spirit comes and fills you with power from heaven." (See

Luke 24:49 NLT.) Jesus knew they would not be in the right frame of mind, and God would not be real to them until the Holy Spirit came upon them and clothed them with power. So they waited, knowing the Holy Spirit must come upon them in order for them to fulfill what Jesus wanted them to do, which was be witnesses to all that had happened to them.

In the second chapter of Acts, the Holy Spirit came upon them. (It would help you to read the second chapter of Acts.) Then came the response on their part. Miracles started happening. People came to Christ. Amazing things started to happen. They were not the initiators. They were the responders.

Jesus wants us to ask for the Holy Spirit to clothe us, because we are the responders, not the initiators. Responding to the Holy Spirit makes the Christian life an amazing adventure.

No longer are you the one trying to make your life with God happen. It's not a self-effort thing. It is responding to a beautiful power that makes God real and removes the self-effort. Jesus said, *"My yoke is easy and My burden is light"* (Matthew 11:30 NKJV). This is what happens when we are propelled by the power from on high.

John, in the book of Revelation, found himself thrust into a strange world – a world called heaven. It was so different than the world he was living in. The world he was living in was a world of persecution, death, injustice, lies, turmoil, prisons, and torture. Then he found himself in a place where God dwells – where God's presence is without limit.

God's presence was shaping everything — heaven was a world molded by His presence. This realm had words for John's generation, words to the church. It was a realm aware of what was going on in our realm, wanting to influence His church. Words of encouragement came from heaven; words of correction came from heaven. Heaven wants to correct what is wrong in our realm. The words were in the form of letters to the seven churches of John's day. These letters were to encourage and correct. (It would be good to read the letters to the seven churches. This is found in Revelation, chapters 2 and 3.)

Heaven is speaking to us today with encouragement and correction. The word at the end of each letter was, "Listen to what the Spirit has to say to the church." So in our day, we must listen to what the Spirit is saying to us. He has personal words for each individual and each church. Sometimes it comes as correction, but that is good. That is how we stay in God's plan. And this is how we change for the better.

Heaven is speaking to us. Jesus is saying, "Look at heaven and compare it to your life. Let your world resemble Mine." Remember, the first thing we are to pray is, *"Thy Kingdom come on earth as it is in heaven."*

Many times I find myself spiritually "dry." I know I can't earn God's presence, but I can ask for it. Luke 11:13 says, *"If you then, evil as you are, know how to give good gifts [gifts that are to their advantage] to your children, how much more will your heavenly Father give the Holy Spirit to those who ask and continue to ask Him!"*

Knowing there is nothing I can do but ask, I begin to ask, continue to ask, and in a couple of days I feel His presence and I am able to move forward. I can't live without His presence, for me it is a necessity.

Jesus said in John 3:6 NKJV, *"That which is born of the flesh is flesh, and that which is born of the Spirit is spirit."* So fleshly striving will not bring the Spirit, but asking will. We can't accomplish things in the flesh that can only be accomplished in the Spirit. The Spirit is the initiator. We are the responders.

There is a worship that has a heavenly sound. I have heard it called "throne room worship." Perhaps you have heard it. It is on a different level than singing about God. It's deep adoration. I feel it resembles the worship around the throne of God. It's a sound that comes from heaven.

The Hallelujah Chorus of Handel's Messiah is what I would call "throne room worship." It was written in 1741 and is still popular today because it strikes a cord in the human heart. The human heart is drawn to the throne room of God because it is where creation came from — where we came from. O God, draw us to your throne room.

Heaven is initiating a lot of things around us. Let us listen and respond. It is a marvelous realm.

WHAT HAVE WE LEARNED FROM THIS CHAPTER?

1. God's presence is what shapes heaven (Revelation 1:10).

2. God is the initiator with His presence. We are the responders.

3. When God's presence comes, we are thrust into another realm, and God becomes real (Acts 2:4).

4. There is nothing I can do to bring God's presence but ask for it (Luke 11:13; Acts 8:14-17).

5. Other Scriptures on the Holy Spirit's presence: Romans 8:15; Galatians 4:6; Ephesians 5:18-20; Acts 10:44-46, 19:6, 11:15-18.

PRAYER

Holy Spirit, we ask You to come and draw us to Jesus. Thank You for coming and drawing me into the presence of God. Without You, my soul is left in the desert. Draw me away from worthless things. Enable me to live in Your presence instead.

THIS IS THE WAY GOD'S KINGDOM,
THE KINGDOM OF HEAVEN, IS. IT IS
ALL AROUND US, YET WE CAN'T SEE IT.
BUT WHEN WE BREATHE IT IN,
IT NOURISHES EVERY CELL
OF OUR BODIES.

CHAPTER 9

THE INVISIBLE
BECOMING VISIBLE

Second Corinthians 4:18 says, "We look not to the things that are seen, but the things that are unseen. For the things that are seen are temporal and fleeting, but the things that are unseen are eternal and everlasting." It's so easy to live in a world that is seen, but the world that is seen is a very small part of our universe. We are only able to observe a fraction of the world we live in. Physicists predict we only see one-half of 1 percent of our natural universe. So to say I only believe in what I see is limiting.

The invisible presence of God permeates everything. Like TV, radio, or cell phones which are being transmitted by invisible electromagnetic waves. As you sit in your room or walk outdoors, there are billions of magnetic waves passing through your body. TV shows, radio shows, cell phone calls – many voices talking, but you hear nothing because you have no receiver. Turn on your radio or TV or cell phone that uses an antenna. It's amazing what you can capture out of the invisible air – an entire world of communication.

God is like that. He may be invisible to our natural eyes, but He has given us the ability to hear Him and receive His presence. Like a radio receiver or cell phone, He has put into man a receiver to know Him and hear Him speaking. It's called our spirit. It's when God talks to us and reveals Himself to us, and when our spirit is turned on to God, it is amazing what we hear. We enter an invisible world that is more real than the world we live in.

As I mentioned before, I grew up an atheist. I ended up praying a simple prayer of inviting Jesus into my life. I opened the door to Him. He came in and turned on the spirit switch. I immediately began to hear His spiritual voice. It happened immediately. I was astonished.

As I talked about in the previous chapter, the pastor at the church where I asked Christ to come into me asked me to pray. I started to pray and could not stop. I had never prayed in my life. After I stopped praying, I looked at the pastor and said, "God wants me to be a missionary." Everyone kind of freaked out because my goal was to be the world's greatest architect. I had just heard the voice of God for the first time. That voice became more familiar as time went on. That voice has become so true and reliable. The voice from heaven has told me things I could have never known on my own.

I had just entered a new world. Jesus calls it being born anew. I was sort of freaked out because I was feeling a force, a presence in my heart I had never felt. But I knew if this was God, then it was the greatest thing that could have ever happened. I began to give it my full attention.

I started to read the Bible and could not stop. This presence inside of me liked me reading the Bible — particularly the New Testament. It was feeding this presence that came inside of me. I was launched into a new world – the world of eternity. I could feel that it was the real world, the world that this world came from.

This presence never left me although I messed up. It began to teach me. It was more than a force or a presence. It was a Person who loved me – loved me so much. He was teaching me to be close to Him and to love Him back with all of my heart. It was Jesus. He is so lovely, so beautiful, fairer than ten thousand.

That same sweet voice I heard when I met Jesus started teaching me, loving me through my mess. My desire is that all humanity could hear this voice from heaven.

Sometimes I cry because of what has happened to me and cry because others can't seem to perceive this marvelous world, knowing that all they are seeking – money and fame – will be taken from them in an hour they know not. It will all be taken, but God is offering us heaven now. A realm that will never be taken from us.

This invisible world, the world where God lives, wants us to perceive it and live in the middle of it. Because He wants us to be with Him. This is what God wants from us just to be with Him. Like the air we breathe, it's invisible, but it is all around us, and we take it in with each breath. It travels to our lungs and then to our blood, nourishing every cell of our bodies. We become alive to God — alive to the God of the universe. It is astounding; we are born into another world, the world where God lives.

This is the way God's kingdom, the kingdom of heaven is. It is all around us, yet we can't see it. But when we breathe it in, it nourishes every cell of our bodies.

Jesus said, *"If anyone thirsts, let him come to Me and drink. He who believes in Me, as the Scripture has said, out of his heart will flow rivers of living water"* (John 7:37-38 NKJV).

The invisible becomes visible!

WHAT HAVE WE LEARNED FROM THIS CHAPTER?

1. Almost everything is invisible. We only see one-half of 1 percent of our universe. The remaining 99.5 percent are invisible forces. Just because they are invisible does not mean they are not real (2 Corinthians 4:18; Hebrews 11:3; Romans 1:20; Colossians 1:15-17).

2. God may be invisible, but He can be seen. God has given us the ability to see Him by giving us His Spirit (John 3:3).

3. God wants us to perceive Him, and He wants to have a love relationship with us, so He makes Himself visible (Colossians 1:15-17; John 14:8-9).

PRAYER

God, I want to see You. I want to see Your glory. Become visible to me — more visible than the world I see; more visible than what I see with my eyes, hear with my ears, touch, or taste. Your world is the real world. Your world is eternal life. Your substance is greater than all. Open my eyes. I will only be whole in Your presence.

WE LAY UP TREASURES IN HEAVEN

BY MAKING CHRIST

OUR TREASURE.

CHAPTER 10

LAY UP TREASURES IN HEAVEN

A gain we will look at our connection with heaven. We are to lay up our treasures in heaven, not earth. So our connection to heaven is real and very active. While we live on earth, we are not to lay up our treasures here for ourselves because they have no value in eternity. And they will all be taken from us at the moment of our death. Jesus said:

"Do not lay up for yourselves treasures on earth, where moth and rust destroy and where thieves break in and steal;

"But lay up for yourselves treasures in heaven, where neither moth nor rust destroys and where thieves do not break in and steal.

"For where your treasure is, there your heart will be also."

Matthew 6:19-21 NKJV

Laying up treasures in heaven is oftentimes seen as something we need to do. Bringing people to Christ, helping people — although this is part of it, I think the way is by valuing God. Jesus said in verse 21, *"Where your treasure is, there your heart will be also."* This is a heart issue.

In heaven, God is treasured above everything. He is so treasured. He is worshiped and adored 24/7. They never stop saying, "Holy, holy, holy is the Lord God, maker of heaven and earth." Jesus is the treasure of heaven. "Treasure" is defined as something of great worth. Something so valuable, so precious, it captures your heart and changes your priorities.

Here are a couple of parables Jesus taught about the kingdom of God. In Matthew 13:44 Jesus said, *"The kingdom of heaven is like something precious buried in a field, which a man found and hid again; then in his joy he goes and sells all he has and buys that field."* This man found something incredibly valuable, so valuable that it made everything he owned so worthless he was willing to sell it ALL to get this one item.

This is the way God and Christ are valued in heaven. They are so valuable, so precious, that everything else is devalued in their presence. The golden streets, the sardius stone, the emeralds are a second thought or no thought because God is the light of heaven. God and His love is the ***treasure*** of heaven.

As God reveals this to our hearts, our treasure is now in heaven — that is how we store up treasures there. He becomes our passion. He occupies our thoughts. He is the love of our lives as that old hymn goes: "The things of earth will grow strangely dim in the light of His glory and grace."

We will follow whatever we value. That can be scary, because there are so many things crying for our attention – not just our attention, but our affection. For God's kingdom to come to earth or in our heart as it is in heaven, God and Christ must be our treasure. I pray that God will take off the blinders from our eyes to where we can see as they see in heaven, and value God as He is valued in heaven.

In Revelation 3:18 Jesus said, *"Therefore I counsel you to purchase from Me gold refined and tested by fire, that you may be [truly] wealthy, and white clothes to clothe you and to keep the shame of your nudity from being seen, and salve to put on your eyes, that you may see."*

This is what we so desperately need in order for our treasure to be in heaven. We desperately need the eyes of heaven to see what the seraphim see and to see what the creatures in heaven see. Christ has sent us the Holy Spirit from heaven to open our eyes to heaven, to make heaven real to us. Jesus said, "He (the Holy Spirit) will take what is Mine and reveal it to you." (See John 16:15.) So we have a Helper to put heaven into our hearts, to take what is going on in heaven and transmit, like an electrical wire, these things to us.

He, the Holy Spirit, will help remove our poverty, help clothe us from our nudity, and provide salve for our eyes so we can see. Obviously, we can't buy these things with money, but Jesus said we can ask for them, for He so desperately wants to give them to us. He so loves us and desperately wants us in a deep relationship with Him.

Jesus said, *"If you then, evil as you are, know how to give good gifts [gifts that are to their advantage] to your children, how much more will your heavenly Father give the Holy Spirit to those who ask and continue to ask Him!"* (Luke 11:13). This is how we purchase from God the things we need – by asking. We can't earn it. We can't be "good enough" or do enough good things. That is a never ending cycle we don't want to get into. We purchase by asking; because Jesus purchased these things for us. But we must ask asking releases heaven into our hearts. When God becomes our greatest treasure, that is how we lay up treasures in heaven. The one thing Jesus wants is for us to be with Him where He is.

WHAT HAVE WE LEARNED FROM THIS CHAPTER?

1. In heaven, God is treasured above everything else.

2. Valuing God, Christ, and the Holy Spirit above all else is a heart issue.

3. Jesus said His kingdom is like a precious treasure, worth selling all you have to get it.

4. We will pursue whatever we value.

5. A Christian must value God above all else or we will be open to many deceptions.

6. We need to ask God to give us the eyes of heaven. *"Buy from me ...salve to put on your eyes, so you can see."* (See Revelation 3:18 NIV).

7. We lay up treasures in heaven by making Christ our treasure.

8. Christ so wants us to treasure Him. Because He loves us so much and wants us to love Him.

PRAYER

Come, Lord Jesus, in all Your glory, into my heart. Thy kingdom come in me just as it is in heaven. As with John in Revelation, let me see Your glory that You may be my greatest treasure. I want You and You alone to be my greatest treasure. Without this, I am open to destructive ways and giving my life to worthless things.

PAUL WAS VERY SPECIFIC IN

1 CORINTHIANS 2:4 THAT IT IS ONLY BY

OR THROUGH THE HOLY SPIRIT THAT WE

CAN SEE OR PERCEIVE GOD.

THE INTELLECT CAN'T GET US THERE.

IT DOES NOT HAVE THE CAPACITY.

CHAPTER 11

THE ABSOLUTE NECESSITY OF THE HOLY SPIRIT IN MAKING HEAVEN REAL

When John saw heaven in the book of Revelation, he said he was in the Spirit, *"[rapt in His power] on the Lord's Day, and I heard behind me a great voice like the calling of a war trumpet"* (Revelation 1:10). It was the Holy Spirit that ushered him into the presence of God and heaven.

Paul was very specific in 1 Corinthians that it is only by or through the Holy Spirit that we can see or perceive God. The intellect can't get us there. It does not have the capacity.

Let's look at 1 Corinthians 2:4 to the end of the chapter in the *New Living Translation*:

"And my message and my preaching were very plain. Rather than using clever and persuasive speeches, I relied only on the power of the Holy Spirit.

"I did this so you would trust not in human wisdom but in the power of God.

"Yet when I am among mature believers, I do speak with words of wisdom, but not the kind of wisdom that belongs to this world or to the rulers of this world, who are soon forgotten.

"No, the wisdom we speak of is the mystery of God – his plan that was previously hidden, even though he made it for our ultimate glory before the world began.

"But the rulers of this world have not understood it; if they had, they would not have crucified our glorious Lord.

"That is what the Scriptures mean when they say, 'No eye has seen, no ear has heard, and no mind has imagined what God has prepared for those who love him.'

"But it was to us that God revealed these things by his Spirit. For his Spirit searches out everything and shows us God's deep secrets.

"No one can know a person's thoughts except that person's own spirit, and no one can know God's thoughts except God's own Spirit.

"And we have received God's Spirit (not the world's spirit), so we can know the wonderful things God has freely given us.

"When we tell you these things, we do not use words that come from human wisdom. Instead, we speak words given

to us by the Spirit, using the Spirit's words to explain spiritual truths.

"But people who aren't spiritual can't receive these truths from God's Spirit. It all sounds foolish to them and they can't understand it, for only those who are spiritual can understand what the Spirit means.

"Those who are spiritual can evaluate all things, but they themselves cannot be evaluated by others.

"For, 'Who can know the Lord's thoughts? Who knows enough to teach him?' But we understand these things, for we have the mind of Christ."

These Scriptures written by Paul leave no doubt that the only way to know God or perceive Him is by way of the Holy Spirit. Our minds were not built to perceive this realm, but the Holy Spirit gives us the ability to perceive God.

Paul says God seems so small through the natural eyes. That is why so many people can't seem to connect. To them, God is a faraway object, an asteroid that is out there, but it has no effect on their lives. Yet others are burning with the love and reality of God. How can this be?

It's the Holy Spirit who makes the difference. Jesus spoke a lot about the absolute necessity of the Holy Spirit.

When Nicodemus came to Jesus at midnight, Nicodemus knew Jesus was from God because of the miracles Jesus was performing. Jesus looked at him, knowing that just outward observation would not be enough for Nicodemus to know what was actually happening. Jesus said to him, "You are going to have to be born again from above." Without this, He could not even see, know, be acquainted with, or experience God.

Let's see what Jesus said:

"Now there was a certain man among the Pharisees named Nicodemus, a ruler (a leader, an authority) among the Jews,

"Who came to Jesus at night and said to Him, Rabbi, we know and are certain that You have come from God [as] a Teacher; for no one can do these signs (these wonderworks, these miracles – and produce the proofs) that You do unless God is with him.

"Jesus answered him, I assure you, most solemnly I tell you, that unless a person is born again (anew, from above), he cannot ever see (know, be acquainted with, and experience) the kingdom of God.

"Nicodemus said to Him, How can a man be born when he is old? Can he enter his mother's womb again and be born?

"Jesus answered, I assure you, most solemnly I tell you, unless a man is born of water and [even] the Spirit, he cannot [ever] enter the kingdom of God.

"What is born of [from] the flesh is flesh [of the physical is physical]; and what is born of the Spirit is spirit.

"Marvel not [do not be surprised, astonished] at My telling you, You must all be born anew (from above).

"The wind blows (breathes) where it wills; and though you hear its sound, yet you neither know where it comes from

nor where it is going. So it is with everyone who is born of the Spirit."

John 3:1-8

Many believers have relied on outward observation to try to find God, using only their intellect. But Jesus is so clear: you can't get there with intellect alone. It will take a power from heaven. We must receive His Spirit to know His reality.

Many have tried to create spiritual reality by natural means – better music, better lighting, better organization, and improved methods using the right words and being relevant. These things might make an improvement and help in the natural realm, but they are of no help in the spiritual realm.

I have led many people in the right prayer to receive Christ only to see no change. God was not becoming real to them. It was only words. The missing ingredient was the Holy Spirit. I cannot explain why the Spirit did not come when they prayed. Perhaps there was something resisting the entrance of the Spirit.

After Paul's conversion, a man named Ananias was instructed by God to find Paul. He entered the house where Paul was. He laid his hands on Saul and said, *"Brother Saul, the Lord Jesus, Who appeared to you along the way by which you came here, has sent me that you may recover your sight and be filled with the Holy Spirit"* (Acts 9:17). It was absolutely necessary for Paul to be filled with the Holy Spirit. It was the Holy Spirit who made all the difference in Paul's life. That ushered him into the realm of God.

At other times, Jesus spoke of the absolute necessity of the Holy Spirit.

When Jesus went into the region of Caesarea Philippi, He asked His disciples:

"Who do people say that the Son of man is?" (Matthew 16:13).

"Simon Peter replied, You are the Christ, the Son of the living God" (Matthew 16:16).

Jesus said, *"Simon Bar-Jonah, For flesh and blood [men] have not revealed this to you, but My Father Who is in heaven"* (v. 17).

Peter was interacting with heaven, and God in heaven was revealing this truth to him from heaven.

God wants to reveal so much to us. He has given us the third person of the Trinity – yes, the Holy Spirit is God.

The Holy Spirit's coming was so essential that Jesus said in John 16:7 that it was good that He was going away, because if He did not, the Holy Spirit would not come. Again, we see that the truth about God can only be revealed by the Holy Spirit from heaven. Jesus said, "My Father in heaven has revealed this to you." God wants to reveal so much to us.

Remember, Jesus said, *"I do not call you servants (slaves) any longer, for the servant does not know what his master is doing (working out). But I have called you My friends, because I have made known to you everything that I have heard from My Father..."* (John 15:15).

Jesus wants to confide in us and tell us everything the Father has told Him. The way this happens is through the Holy Spirit. *"He* (the Holy Spirit) *will take of (receive, draw upon) what is Mine and will reveal (declare, disclose, transmit) it to you"* (John 16:14).

How do we receive this marvelous Spirit that opens heaven and opens the realm of God and His voice to us? We receive it when we invite Jesus to come live in our house (which is our bodies); our awareness of Him becomes greater as we ask for Him to reveal Himself to us. The Holy Spirit makes Him real. Asking is the way forward:

> *"If you then, evil as you are, know how to give good gifts [gifts that are to their advantage] to your children, how much more will your heavenly Father give the Holy Spirit to those who ask and continue to ask Him!"* (Luke 11:13)

We can't do enough good deeds, can't fast enough, or pray enough to earn the Holy Spirit. All through Scripture, the Holy Spirit is said to be a gift, not something we can earn. (See Acts 11:17.) So all we can do is ask for the Holy Spirit; then respond to His presence and His voice.

Oftentimes, I become spiritually dry and feel disconnected from God. I don't start trying to earn His presence. I start asking, and usually in about three days I feel the Holy Spirit, the conscious presence returns. He did not leave; I just lost contact with His conscious presence. I can't live without feeling His presence. I absolutely love Him and His nearness to me. Sensing His presence makes everything in my life work.

God wants to reveal so much to us through His Spirit. Jesus said we are His friends, and He wants to continue to tell us everything the Father has told Him. This is astounding. When we come to Christ, we don't get a secondhand relationship — a hand-me-down relationship. We receive from Jesus everything He receives from the Father. Jesus said, "I have loved you as much as the Father has loved Me." (John 15:9) Not hand-me-down love but the same love.

Jesus wants to pull us close and reveal His heart to us. Let's let it happen. There is nothing in this life that is more important than being God's companion. Everything else will fail us; this will not. But we must ask for this relationship. We can't earn it; we ask God for it.

WHAT HAVE WE LEARNED FROM THIS CHAPTER?

1. We must have the Holy Spirit to perceive God. (John 15:26, 16:14).

2. Our intellect will not connect us to God. Only the Holy Spirit can connect us. (John 14:15-17, 26; 1 Corinthians 2:14).

3. Jesus calls us His friend! (John 15:15).

4. Jesus wants to reveal to us EVERYTHING the Father has shown Him. (John 15:15).

5. The way to receive this wonderful word God wants to reveal to us is by asking.

PRAYER

Jesus, You have taught us to ask for the Holy Spirit in order for the kingdom of God to be real. We can't see Your realm without the Holy Spirit. So today we ask for the presence of the Holy Spirit so we can see. Like a blind man, we are desperate to see.

Note: In Mark 10:46 to 52, there is a wonderful story about a blind man named Bartimaeus. He was a blind beggar. When he heard about Jesus, he began to shout, "Son of David, have pity and mercy on me [now]!" Many people around him "severely censured and reproved him, telling him to keep still, but he kept on shouting out all the more." When God puts an intense hunger for Jesus in our hearts, there may be people around you who don't understand and will ask you to be quiet. They may tell you that you already have all God wants to do in your life. So just calm down. This is NOT true; there is more God wants to show us — there is a deeper relationship with Him that is available. Ask God to give you a hunger for more. When Jesus heard Bartimaeus shouting, He stopped, told the crowd to bring him to me. Bartimaeus threw off his beggars clothes and came to Jesus. Then Jesus made an incredible, powerful statement. He said, "What do you want Me to do for you?" I feel Jesus is asking us this same question. Remember, it was Bartimaeus' boldness and his desperation that made Jesus single him out from the crowd. Jesus loves boldness and desperation.

THE EARLY CHURCH RELIED HEAVILY
ON THE HOLY SPIRIT SPEAKING
TO THEM. ALL THROUGH THE BOOK
OF ACTS, THE HOLY SPIRIT WAS
SPEAKING TO THEM, GIVING
DIRECTION AND COUNSELING THEM.

CHAPTER 12

ABSOLUTE NECESSITY TO HEAR THE HOLY SPIRIT (A VOICE FROM HEAVEN)

In the previous chapter, we talked about the absolute necessity to receive the Holy Spirit. Without the Holy Spirit, we can't even perceive God properly. We can't understand God, and as Jesus said, "Without the Holy Spirit, we can't even enter the kingdom of God." (See John 3:5.)

The human intellect can't conceive of the things of God. It's like when you talk to your dog or cat and they look at you like, "I don't speak your language, and my understanding is very limited." This is the state we find ourselves in with God, but He has given us the Holy Spirit so we can see, hear, and taste the things of God.

Yes, we are given spiritual eyesight, spiritual taste, and spiritual ears to perceive this marvelous kingdom that is invisible to the natural senses, but so visible to the Holy Spirit. One of the great things we are given is the ability to hear the Holy Spirit talk to us. That has been one of the greatest mysteries in my life — hearing the Holy Spirit. Sometimes it is a soft voice, and sometimes it is a download.

It can be very astonishing when things are told to me in exact detail. Then I watch them happen exactly as the Holy Spirit told me.

I had a friend who had stage 4 melanoma cancer. He had hundreds of tumors in his body. He went to some of the best cancer hospitals in the country and was told there was no cure. So he went home to die.

His wife did not accept the doctors' conclusions, but prayed diligently. She would not give up. My wife and I prayed diligently, but our friends said we needed to prepare her for the inevitable. We kept praying in spite of what everyone was saying.

Then one night just before falling asleep, the Holy Spirit spoke to me – not in an audible voice, but in a spiritual download. He told me in detail what would happen to my friend. He told me that there was an experimental treatment. He would find the treatment, and his cancer would be cured. He was about a month or two from death.

When I got up the next day, I knew for sure it was the Holy Spirit. No words can describe the spiritual feeling that came over me. I called them and told them what I had heard in the night. I don't think they believed me.

I watched the whole thing unfold. He went to a doctor the next week. He told him there was an experimental treatment in California that was only taking terminally ill patients. I knew then that that was what the Holy Spirit had told me.

They did not have the money to pay for the treatments, and the insurance said they didn't cover experimental treatment. His wife appealed to the insurance company, we prayed, and the insurance company miraculously changed their mind.

Next, they did not have the money to fly to California. His wife asked an airline if they could fly them for free. The airline agreed, so they were on their way. I was on the sideline saying, "That's it."

He began to take the treatment immediately. His tumors began to shrink until hundreds were gone. Today he has not one active tumor in his body, and that was ten years ago.

That experience woke me up! I realized the Holy Spirit can speak to us and wants to speak to us. I became desperate to hear. What I viewed as a casual thing before became a heart cry, "God, I want to hear Your voice."

The Bible is filled with exhortations to hear the Holy Spirit. In the book of Revelation after each letter written to the seven churches, there is this exhortation: *"He who is able to hear, let him listen to and give heed to what the Spirit says to the assemblies (churches). To him who overcomes (is victorious), I will grant to eat [of the fruit] of the tree of life, which is in the paradise of God"* (Revelation 2:7, 11, 17, 29; 3:6, 13, 22).

Jesus talked a lot about hearing. In Matthew 11:15 Jesus said, *"He who has ears to hear, let him be listening...."* In John 10:27 Jesus said, *"The sheep that are My own hear and are listening to My voice; and I know them, and they follow Me."*

In John 16, Jesus began teaching on the Holy Spirit. In verse 13 He said:

"But when He, the Spirit of Truth (the Truth-giving Spirit) comes, He will guide you into all the Truth (the whole, full Truth). For He will not speak His own message [on His own authority]; but He will tell whatever He hears [from the Father; He will give the message that has been given to Him], and He will announce and declare to you the things that are to come [that will happen in the future]."

This is Jesus speaking about the Holy Spirit. Look at the words He is using about the Spirit: He will speak, tell, announce, and declare. The Holy Spirit is speaking, telling, announcing, and declaring. This is wonderful news; we are not alone. Let's listen.

The early church relied heavily on the Holy Spirit speaking to them. All through the book of Acts, the Holy Spirit was speaking to them, giving direction and counseling them.

Many scholars call the book of Acts "the acts of the Holy Spirit." The Holy Spirit is mentioned seventy times in the book of Acts.

Let's look at some examples of how the Holy Spirit spoke to the early church. I will only briefly talk about these events. It would be good for you to take these Scriptures and study them more fully.

In Acts 8, verses 27-29 we read:

"So he got up and went. And behold, an Ethiopian, a eunuch of great authority under Candace the queen of the Ethiopians, who was in charge of all her treasure, had come to Jerusalem to worship.

"And he was [now] returning, and sitting in his chariot he was reading the book of the prophet Isaiah.

"Then the [Holy] Spirit said to Philip, Go forward and join yourself to this chariot."

Philip explained the passage the Ethiopian was reading was *"like a sheep He was led to the slaughter, and as a lamb before its shearer is dumb, so he opens not His mouth"* (v. 32). Philip explained the passage to the Ethiopian that it was Christ. The Ethiopian immediately wanted to accept Jesus as the Messiah. They stopped the chariot, and he was baptized. This encounter may be why Ethiopia was one of the first, if not the first Christian nation, and is predominantly Christian today. This encounter happened because the Holy Spirit spoke to Philip and guided him to the Ethiopian.

Again, in the book of Acts, Paul was in Antioch. *"While they were worshiping the Lord and fasting, the Holy Spirit said, Separate now for Me Barnabas and Saul for the work to which I have called them...So then, being sent out by the Holy Spirit, they went down to Seleucia, and from [that port] they sailed away to Cyprus"* (Acts 13:2,4).

So continued Paul's travels, preaching and sharing the Word of God in synagogues and marketplaces of other nations.

The Holy Spirit so loves to speak to us. There are so many examples; I will briefly mention a few more. You can study these as we go along this journey.

Peter had a vision about the Gentiles. Acts 10:19 states, *"And while Peter was earnestly revolving the vision in his mind and meditating on it, the [Holy] Spirit said to him, Behold, three men are looking for you!"* This led to an amazing encounter with the Gentiles where Peter got to tell in detail about Jesus. *"While Peter was still speaking these words, the Holy Spirit fell on all who were listening to the message"* (Acts 10:44). (Please read this for yourself. It is found in the tenth chapter of Acts.)

This led to the door being opened to the Gentiles. Again, it was the Holy Spirit speaking. These two events we just read had huge implications and changed the course of Christianity. They were all directed by the Holy Spirit. At other times, they were forbidden by the Holy Spirit to go to certain places, and they were sent to other places by the Holy Spirit. (Read Acts, chapter 16.)

In the book of Acts, close to the end of the book, the Holy Spirit is telling Paul he will be imprisoned and will suffer. (See Acts 20:22-23.)

The book of Acts ends with Paul saying:

"The Holy Spirit was right in saying through Isaiah the prophet to your forefathers:

"Go to this people and say to them, You will indeed hear and hear with your ears but will not understand, and you will indeed look and look with your eyes but will not see [not perceive, have knowledge of or become acquainted with what you look at, at all].

"For the heart (the understanding, the soul) of this people has grown dull (stupid, hardened, and calloused), and their ears are heavy and hard of hearing and they have shut tight their eyes, so that they may not perceive and have knowledge and become acquainted with their eyes and hear with their ears and understand with their souls and turn [to Me and be converted], that I may heal them."

Acts 28:25-27

This is how the book of Acts ends with the statement the Holy Spirit was right in saying. The Holy Spirit is speaking to us today. It is vital that we listen. If we don't, we are going to end up in the wrong direction.

When Jesus looked at the people, it says He was moved with pity and sympathy for them because they were bewildered (harassed and distressed and helpless) like sheep without a shepherd. Matthew 9:36.

Christ has come to shepherd us in love by the Holy Spirit. Let's let Him do it.

God, my ears are attentive to You as my first love. *"He who has an ear, let him hear what the Spirit says to the churches"* (Revelation 2:29 NKJV).

It is so exciting that we can actually hear the voice of God. It is the greatest excitement we could ever have. Remember the Holy Spirit comes to us in greater ways as we ask the Father to send Him to us. James 5:16 tells us that tremendous power is released through the passionate, heartfelt prayer. If we want to experience God on a deeper level, heartfelt, passionate prayer is the way forward.

WHAT HAVE WE LEARNED FROM THIS CHAPTER?

1. Without the Holy Spirit, we can't even perceive God or understand Him.

2. God has given us the Holy Spirit so we can taste, see, and hear God.

3. God is invisible to the natural senses, but visible by the Holy Spirit.

4. We can hear the Holy Spirit speak to us.

5. The Bible exhorts us to hear the Holy Spirit.

6. The early church relied heavily on the voice of the Holy Spirit. Acts 10:19, 13:2-4, 15:28, 16:6-7, 21:11.

7. He who has ears, let him hear what the Spirit is saying to the church. (Revelation 2:7, 2:11, 2:17, 2:29, 3:6, 3:13, 3:22.)

8. Persistent, heartfelt prayer is the way forward (James 5:16).

9. Read the parable of the friend at midnight (Luke 11:5-8). Persistence is what makes the difference.

PRAYER

Holy Spirit, You are my lifeline. Without You, I can't see or understand God. You allow me to see the face of God. You make Him so real. Through You, I can experience God. Oh God, we want to be one with You, so close we can hear Your heart beating. We want to be like John the Beloved, or Mary sitting at Your feet. Nothing else is more important. Deliver me from anything that is less than this. This is the highest peak of the mountain I must climb. All other mountains are just valleys or illusionary mountains.

Note: God is wanting to do so so much in our lives. We cannot get there on our own; we need His powerful help. We can't even see it without His help. He is ready to answer our prayers; all we need to do is persistently ask. It's not what we can do for Him. It's what He wants to do in us. He loves us so much and wants our love and companionship.

We must refuse to think of heaven
as just a future event when we die.
We must see heaven as here now,
surrounding us as we go through life
on earth. This perspective will have a
profound effect on our
relationship with God, Christ,
the Holy Spirit, and the heavenly
realm. Earth realm was never
designed to operate on its own,
separated from God.

CHAPTER 13

HEAVEN IS A PRESENT REALITY

As we have been studying in the Lord's Prayer, the first thing we are to pray is, *"Your kingdom come, Your will be done on earth as it is in heaven"* (Matthew 6:10). This is telling us that the kingdom of heaven is to come to earth to live in our hearts.

As we saw in the chapters before this, we are to interact with heaven in this life. The Holy Spirit came from heaven and has invaded our hearts and makes heaven real to us. We are to ask for the realm of heaven to come to our hearts and to be established there – for the substance of heaven to descend into our hearts. This is not just doctrine or a belief. Something actually happens. The substance of God comes into us and changes our DNA. We become citizens of a new realm – heaven.

It is so difficult to communicate this because it is a supernatural encounter that can only be communicated by the Holy Spirit. The natural human mind can't grasp it.

We must refuse to think of heaven as just a future event when we die. We must see heaven as here now, surrounding us as we go through life on earth. This perspective will have a profound effect on our relationship with God, Christ, the Holy Spirit, and the heavenly realm.

In the book of Hebrews, the author contrasts the Old Covenant with the New Covenant and shows why the New Covenant is so much better. In Hebrews 12:21-24, we see this stark contrast between the Old and the New:

"In fact, so awful and terrifying was the [phenomenal] sight that Moses said, I am terrified (aghast and trembling with fear).

"But rather, you have come to Mount Zion, even to the city of the living God, the heavenly Jerusalem, and to countless multitudes of angels in festal gathering,

"And to the church (assembly) of the Firstborn who are registered [as citizens] in heaven, and to the God Who is Judge of all, and to the spirits of the righteous (the redeemed in heaven) who have been made perfect,

"And to Jesus, the Mediator (Go-between, Agent) of a new covenant, and to the sprinkled blood which speaks [of mercy], a better and nobler and more gracious message than the blood of Abel [which cried out for vengeance]."

The writer of Hebrews says, "But rather, you have come." This is present tense. It is happening now. We have come now to Mount Zion, which represents the dwelling place of God. It says you have now come to the city of the living God, the heavenly Jerusalem. You have now come to countless multitudes of angels in festive gatherings and to the church of the Firstborn who are registered citizens in heaven. We have now come to God and to the spirits of the righteous (the redeemed in heaven) who have been made perfect, and to Jesus and to the sprinkled blood.

It would be good for us to spend some time thinking about these verses because this is the world we are now living in. This is our real reality. The key words are, "You have come." That means all that is happening in this verse is happening now.

It would be good to close your eyes and visualize these things. See yourself there in heaven before the throne of God, surrounded by lightning, thunder, and angels' voices. You are there conversing with God and Christ about the things that concern you, and He is sharing with you about the things that are concerning Him.

This is our real reality because this is so amazing, so powerful, and because the Trinity so desperately wants us to live here. God so wants us to dwell in His realm because we are the object of His great love. This comes with a warning. Things that are extremely valuable come with a warning, like a label that reads, "Be careful with this. It is extremely valuable. Don't neglect to take special care."

This warning is to see that you don't reject Him or refuse to listen to Him who speaks to you now (Hebrews 12:25).

Remember in Revelation 2:7 where Jesus spoke these words: *"He who is able to hear, let him listen to and give heed to what the Spirit says to the assemblies (churches)...."* I think my biggest sin is I am not listening to what the Spirit of God is saying to me. We are busy with other things. We have filled our lives and minds with things that in the end will not matter one bit. They are only temporary entertainment with no value, and we will grow tired of them in time.

The God of the universe is speaking to you right now. We must get quiet, stop the "merry-go-round," and listen. What we will hear will be so amazing we will say, "Why did I not do this earlier?"

On a previous night, I was praying for a friend who was in trouble. I got in bed, getting ready to go to sleep. I started to picture myself before the throne of God. God the Father was there. Jesus was there. I just walked in like I belonged. I was very comfortable being there.

Remembering the words of Jesus, "I no longer call you servants but friends, because I have made known to you everything I have heard from My Father." (See John 15:15.) I saw Jesus as a friend, and He was confiding in me, telling me things that were on His heart. I felt like there were things He wanted to discuss with me, but I could not hear that clearly.

I began to talk to Him about my friend, asking Him to help him. Then I drifted off to sleep.

The next day, a major breakthrough happened in my friend's life, a huge breakthrough.

This is our reality. This is how it really is. I want to live there. Somehow it felt like this was the place Jesus had purchased for me, like this was my true home.

This can be hard to grasp.

The God of the universe wants to be with us and talk to us. He wants to love us. He wants us to hear His heart, and He wants to hear our heart. This is why Jesus came. This is why He died on the cross – to give us this place.

Jesus did not die just to forgive us of our sins — He forgave us of our sins so we could have a close relationship with Him.

WHAT HAVE WE LEARNED FROM THIS CHAPTER?

1. Heaven is not just a future event, but a present event.

    - Hebrews 12:22

    - Colossians 3:1

    - Luke 17:20-21

    - Matthew 3:1-2

    - Matthew 12:28

    - Luke 2:13-15

2. Jesus has called us His friend and wants to share His heart with us.

   - John 15:15

3. The verses in Hebrews 12:21-29 come with a warning. The warning is not to reject Him or refuse to listen to Him who is speaking to you <u>now</u>.

   - Hebrews 12:25

   - Hebrews 2:1-3

   - Matthew 11:15

   - Matthew 13:9

   - Matthew 13:43

   - Revelation 2:7

   - Revelation 2:17

   - Revelation 2:11

   - Revelation 3:12-13

   - Revelation 3:21-22

   - Revelation 13:9

4. Not hearing the voice of God in Scripture and by the Spirit can be dangerous. It can leave us open to deception within and throughout.

PRAYER

God, help me to hear Your voice. I need Your help. Help me not to be so busy. Help me to be quiet and listen to You. You are my number one treasure, and I want to hear from You.

GOD HAS PROVIDED US A TRANSPORTING

AGENT. JESUS SAID THAT THE HOLY SPIRIT

WOULD BE THAT TRANSPORTING VEHICLE.

IN JOHN 16:14 JESUS SAID,

"HE (THE HOLY SPIRIT) *WILL HONOR*

AND GLORIFY ME, BECAUSE HE WILL

TAKE OF (RECEIVE, DRAW UPON)

WHAT IS MINE AND WILL REVEAL

(DECLARE, DISCLOSE, TRANSMIT) IT TO YOU."

CHAPTER **14**

ROLE OF THE HOLY SPIRIT IN BRINGING THE KINGDOM OF GOD

As we have been studying, the first thing we are to ask for in the Lord's Prayer is, "Thy kingdom come on earth as it is in heaven," and the place on earth the kingdom is to come is in our hearts, for God sets up His kingdom within us. This is so wonderful just as the booming voice from the throne of God says: The dwelling place of God is with men. (*See* Revelation 21:3.

The place God wants to dwell is in our hearts (the center of our being). He wants to be as close to us as possible. He wants to be one with us. Absolutely no separation.

So when we pray, "Thy kingdom come on earth as it is in heaven," what we are really asking is for one realm, heaven, to be transported to another realm, our hearts. In order for that to happen, there must be a transporting agent. Like a truck or a ship, they transport goods from one part of the world to another.

God has provided us a transporting agent. Jesus said that the Holy Spirit would be that transporting vehicle. In John 16:14 Jesus said, *"He (the Holy Spirit) will honor and glorify Me, because He will take of (receive, draw upon) what is Mine and will reveal (declare, disclose, transmit) it to you. Everything that the Father has is Mine. That is what I meant when I said that He, the Spirit, will take the things that are Mine and will reveal (declare, disclose, transmit) it to you."* (John 16:14-15).

So Jesus is saying that the Holy Spirit is the transmitting agent. So when we pray, "Thy kingdom come," we are asking for the Holy Spirit from heaven to come and bring heaven to us, to transport heaven to us.

As I said before, whenever I get spiritually dry and God seems distant, which can happen often, I stop and begin to ask for the Holy Spirit from heaven to come. Usually, after about three days His conscious presence comes. Jesus encourages us to ask for the Holy Spirit to come, knowing that without His presence, heaven will seem like a faraway land, and earth will seem like the only reality. Remember, the Holy Spirit comes from heaven.

In Luke 11:13 Jesus said, *"If you then, evil as you are, know how to give good gifts [gifts that are to their advantage] to your children, how much more will your heavenly Father give the Holy Spirit to those who ask and continue to ask Him!"*

Jesus is likening the Holy Spirit to a precious gift, like when you give gifts to your children on Christmas morning, knowing how excited they will be. You get such pleasure watching them tear open the hidden treasures you have bought them. Their excitement brings us so much pleasure. That's one of the things I loved about Christmas — watching our children as they grew up opening presents.

Now I get to watch our precious grandchildren's excitement at Christmas. My wife and I buy way too much, but Jesus says, "How much more will the heavenly Father give the Holy Spirit." The emphasis here is *how much more to those who ask and continue to ask.*

God has that same attitude. He gets such pleasure and gets so excited when we ask for the Holy Spirit, knowing that when we open His present, great joy, great pleasure, great wonder, and revelation will come to us. Intimacy will be the result.

In Luke 12:32 Jesus said, *"Do not be seized with alarm and struck with fear, little flock, for it is your Father's good pleasure to give you the kingdom!"*

WHAT HAVE WE LEARNED FROM THIS CHAPTER?

1. When we pray the Lord's Prayer, we are praying for the kingdom (the kingdom of God) to be transferred to another kingdom (our hearts).

2. The Holy Spirit is the transporting agent like a train or a ship transporting goods from one part of the world to another (John 16:14).

3. The Holy Spirit will reveal the things of God to us supernaturally.

4. When we pray for the conscious presence of the Holy Spirit, God becomes real (Luke 11:13).

5. It is God's great pleasure to give us the kingdom, which is His tangible presence (Luke 12:32).

6. The kingdom of God is the presence of God in our hearts.

7. In R.T. Kendall's Book, *The Sermon on the Mount*, he defines the kingdom of God: "the kingdom is the immediate, direct, and conscious witness of the Holy Spirit. It is God's conscious presence and enabling grace."

PRAYER

Holy Spirit, come. I want the kingdom of heaven to be more real to me than the physical world I live in. This is Your purpose, Your role in the earth. So again we say, come!

God's love for us is intense. His desire to be with us is intense. From Genesis to Revelation, God's desire has been to be one with us. Let's yield to Jesus' desire, make Him our number one passion, and be done with lesser things that eat away our time with Him.

CHAPTER 15

JOHN, CHAPTER 17

L et's now look at John, chapter 17. It would be good for you to read over it before we continue in this chapter. This is the last prayer Jesus prayed before He was betrayed by Judas and arrested. If you were about to leave your best friends whom you loved so so much, if you were not going to see them for a while and you had a final prayer, you would pour out your heart.

This prayer is amazing because you hear the heart of Jesus. Here He states His innermost desires. Knowing His desires will bring a great closeness to Him. Like when a friend shares their innermost longings, a closeness is the result. Also, knowing Jesus' desires will give us direction in our relationship with Him.

Let's start toward the end of the prayer. Here Jesus declares His heart in John 17:24:

"Father, I desire that they also whom You have entrusted to Me [as Your gift to Me] may be with Me where I am, so that they may see My glory, which You have given Me [Your love gift to Me]; for You loved Me before the foundation of the world."

Here Jesus is stating His overwhelming desire. The Greek word used here for "desire" is an intense word. We could use the word "passion." This passionate desire is pointed toward us. We are the object of His desire. He wants us to be with Him. This is the whole reason He came. This is the reason for the cross.

If we think of that booming voice of Revelation 21:3, it says, "The dwelling place of God is with men." This is the passionate cry from the throne room of God. This is the cry of God to us. This desire for us to be with Him is not just a future event, but a now event. He longs for us to be with Him now. He has made all the provisions for this to happen now. He can't wait for a future event. His desire is for us now.

God sent the Holy Spirit to come and live on the inside of us. The Spirit of Jesus was never satisfied with the relationship He had with His disciples. They only knew Him on the outside, perceiving Him through sight and sound. His desire was to come on the inside of them and us and for us to be one spirit with Him. He wanted us to really know Him, to really love Him with all of our hearts, all of our soul, and all of our mind and strength.

He wants us to talk together, have conversations, fellowship, be in the same room together, love each other, to be companions because we are the bride of Christ.

God's love for us is intense. His desire to be with us is intense. From Genesis to Revelation, God's desire has been to be one with us. Let's yield to Jesus' desire, make Him our number one passion, and be done with lesser things that eat away our time with Him. Let's look to Him and say, "I am in. Give me the strength to love You the way You have loved me." This and this alone is the ultimate purpose of life – the only thing that will ultimately satisfy our heart. It is the only thing that will make sense in the end. Everything else is like grass that withers in the hot sun.

In John 17:24, Jesus prayed that they may see His glory. He so badly wants us to see Him for who He is. The definition of "glory" or "to glorify" is to reveal who that person or thing really is by stating who they really are and praising and honoring who they really are. It is revealing and uncovering that person or thing. Jesus so desires us to see Him for who He really is. If we really get a glimpse of His glory, who He really is, we will be undone! Like the prophet Isaiah when he saw the Lord high and lifted up. He was undone. This glory would ruin us for cold and casual Christianity. Jesus was not casual about the cross. God, help us shake off our coldness and our casualness. Seeing Him for who He is will ruin us.

There is so much in this prayer in John 17. It is so wonderful that this prayer was recorded. In this prayer, Jesus defines eternal life: *"And this is eternal life: [it means] to know (to perceive, recognize, become acquainted with, and understand) You, the only true and real God, and [likewise] to know Him, Jesus [as the] Christ (the Anointed One, the Messiah), Whom You have sent"* (John 17:3).

Again, Jesus is showing that knowing Him and the Father is the ultimate goal of God, that even eternal life can't be separated from being one with Him. It's not just a prayer we pray, but having intimate knowledge of God by the indwelling Holy Spirit is what eternal life is. Being one with Christ is the very definition of eternal life.

This prayer is so amazing; let's look at verse 21. Jesus prays and makes an astonishing statement: *"That they all may be one, [just] as You, Father, are in Me and I in You, that they also may be one in Us, so that the world may believe and be convinced that You have sent Me."*

The Father, the Son, and the Holy Spirit are one by nature. They are God united by divine substance. They are the same substance, blending together in divineness. They love each other, submit themselves to each other, and are in total harmony. Jesus prayed they (meaning you and me) would be one, just as He, God, and the Holy Spirit are one. Jesus is praying that we would be one in the same way. *"Just as You, Father, are in Me and I in You."* So Jesus is saying that we will be one by Jesus being in us, giving us His divine nature, uniting us with God.

As Peter said in 2 Peter 1:4, that we would become *"sharers (partakers) of the divine nature."* In John 17:23, Jesus says this is how oneness is achieved: *"I in them and You in Me in order that they may become one (in us.)"*

Look at what Jesus said: He said I will be in you (supernaturally) and you will be in Me (supernaturally) this is a divine mystery. This is Jesus' ultimate desire. His whole purpose.

Jesus actually comes on the inside of us and we actually go on the inside of Him. United together in love, forever.

We don't become one with one another because we decide it would be a good idea. We tried that, and it does not work. We are like water, and God is like oil. We just don't mix no matter how hard you shake it. It keeps separating. God's solution was to come inside of us and give us His divine nature, replacing the water with oil. Now we mix.

Our union with Christ must be supernatural. Jesus called it being born anew from above. So is our union with each other. It must be supernatural. God is inviting us to be one with Him, one with the Son, and the Holy Spirit. We are being invited into a relationship with them. They are dwelling inside of us, and we are being invited to dwell inside of them. God has not given us an inferior relationship. Jesus said, "I have loved you as much as the Father has loved Me." (*See* John 15). Our relationship with God does not get downgraded as it travels to us from the Godhead. We are given the same love the Father has for the Son.

This is so astonishing it demands our total attention, because we are not dealing with church or religion, but with God who made a billion galaxies, with a billion stars, and billions and billions of everything.

And we are being invited to live with them and to live in them. This may sound crazy, but this is what Jesus was constantly talking about. He did not come to establish another religion; His purpose was for us to dwell inside Him, and for Him to dwell inside us. Everything else in "Christianity" should flow from this. Living inside God, and God living inside us. This is the purpose, this is the core, this is the desire of Jesus. Oneness on a level that is unimaginable. The Father, Son, and Holy Spirit are inviting us into fellowship with them. This is amazing.

I pray that God will allow us to see this marvelous invitation, this marvelous glory; give us the eyes to see it and ears to hear it and then the power to pursue it!

WHAT HAVE WE LEARNED FROM THIS CHAPTER?

1. In this prayer, Jesus is revealing to us His greatest desires.

2. Jesus' greatest passionate desire is that we would be with Him where He is.

3. We are the object of His desires.

4. The persistent cry from the throne of God and the booming voice from heaven is that He wants to dwell with us.

5. Dwelling with God is not a future event. It is for us now.

6. Jesus wants us to see His glory. Then we will truly know who He is; and when we realize who He is, we will be undone.

7. Knowing Him intimately is the very definition of eternal life. Jesus' desire is that we be ONE with Him, us

living inside Him and Him living inside us — like two substances mixing together — never to be separated.

8. We are invited into fellowship with the Trinity. Father, Son and Holy Spirit and You. The Trinity fellowships with One Another and we are invited to participate in that fellowship.

PRAYER

We ask You, God, for spiritual eyes to see and ears to hear. Open to us this marvelous world that is beyond anything we could dream of. Rescue us from lesser things that we may see Your glory, so we may be one with You as You are one with the Father, Son, and the Holy Spirit, because this is Your number one pursuit. Make this miracle happen inside me. Holy Spirit, come by your miraculous power, and complete this supernatural event inside of me. You, Holy Spirit, are the only one that can accomplish this in us. Give me eyes to see it, ears to hear it, and the supernatural ability to enter into you.

"SO I SAY TO YOU, ASK AND KEEP ON ASKING
AND IT SHALL BE GIVEN YOU; SEEK AND KEEP
ON SEEKING AND YOU SHALL FIND; KNOCK
AND KEEP ON KNOCKING AND THE DOOR
SHALL BE OPENED TO YOU.
"FOR EVERYONE WHO ASKS AND KEEPS ON
ASKING RECEIVES; AND HE WHO SEEKS AND
KEEPS ON SEEKING FINDS; AND TO HIM
WHO KNOCKS AND KEEPS ON KNOCKING,
THE DOOR SHALL BE OPENED."

LUKE 11:9-10

CHAPTER 16

WHEN GOD BECOMES REAL

We have started most of these chapters with the Lord's Prayer. The first thing we are to pray for is, *"Your kingdom come on earth as it is in heaven."* This is such an awesome prayer because we are asking for His kingdom, the kingdom of heaven, to become real to us and to actually live in us — for the kingdom of heaven to enter our hearts, to come to us, and live in us.

I work a lot with youth. One of the things that breaks my heart is that God is not real to them. They believe all the right doctrines and attend youth group, but it is just head knowledge. They know Scriptures and can quote them. You ask, "Are you a Christian?" and the response is, "Yes." But as you inquire further, God is not real. He is just a "worldview," a way to think. They think being a Christian is being a good person, loving others, and staying away from the worst sins of murder, robbery, or beating people up.

The way God has set things up is for Him to become real, more real than the world around us. For me, when the Holy Spirit entered my heart, God became real. No argument, no doctoral word had convinced me. God had to become real, and the Holy Spirit made Him real to me. God made Himself real to me. Like Paul on the Damascus road, no argument could have convinced him that he did not meet Jesus! His theology was set in stone until God became real to him. Jesus showed up to him in person. (Read Acts, chapter 9.)

There are people all over the world having personal encounters with Jesus. You hear their testimonies all the time on the internet. All through the Bible you read about these encounters: from Isaiah seeing the Lord high and lifted up, to Paul going to the third heaven, to John on the Isle of Patmos being ushered into heaven. These encounters changed the course of these men and women's lives, and God became real. These are real encounters with a real God.

Like I said before, much of the Bible was experiences people had with God, then they would record those experiences. From an angel coming to Mary, to Jesus telling Peter, "Flesh and blood did not reveal this to you, but My Father in heaven revealed this to you," God reached down from heaven, touching Peter's spirit, and Jesus became real at that moment. (see Matthew 16:17.)

The cry of my heart is that God would become more real. This is why so many people are more interested in everything else other than God, because they see the world around them as real and God as a belief system. You want to live in the world that is real to you.

One of my favorite stories about God becoming real comes from Charles G. Finney. He was a great Presbyterian preacher who was a leader in the second great awakening during the 1830s. He was a lawyer and a skeptic. He decided to settle once and for all if Jesus Christ was real. So he became serious about Christ. He began to pray a lot, and his seriousness and his prayers led him to this experience:

"As I went in and shut the door after me, it seemed as if I met the Lord Jesus Christ face to face. It did not occur to me then, nor did it for some time afterward, that it was wholly a mental state. On the contrary, it seemed to me that I met him face to face, and saw him as I would see any other man. He said nothing, but looked at me in such a manner as to break me right down at his feet. I have always since regarded this as a most remarkable state of mind; for it seemed to me a reality that he stood before me, and that I fell down at his feet and poured out my soul to him. I wept aloud like a child, and made such confessions as I could with my choked utterance. It seemed to me as if I bathed his feet with my tears; and yet I had no distinct impression that I touched him, that I recollect. I must have continued in this state for a good while; but my mind was too much absorbed with the interview to recollect scarcely anything that I said.

But I know as soon as my mind became calm enough to break off from the interview, I returned to the front office and found that the fire that I had just made of large wood was nearly burned out. But as I returned and was about to take a seat by the fire, I received a mighty baptism of the Holy Ghost. Without expecting it, without ever having the thought in my mind that there was any such thing for me, without any recollection that I had ever heard the thing mentioned by any person in the world, at a moment entirely unexpected by me, the Holy Spirit descended upon me in a manner that seemed to go through me, body and soul. I could feel the impression, like a wave of electricity, going through and through me. Indeed it seemed to come in waves, and waves of liquid love: — for I could not express it in any other way. And yet it did not seem like water, but rather as the breath of God. I can recollect distinctly that it seemed to fan me; like immense wings; and it seemed to me, as these waves passed over me, that they literally moved my hair like a passing breeze.

No words can express the wonderful love that was shed abroad in my heart. It seemed to me that I should burst. I wept aloud with joy and love; and I do not know but I should say I literally bellowed out the unutterable gushings of my heart. These waves came over me, and over me, and over me one after the other, until I recollect and I cried out, "I shall die if these waves continue to pass over me." I said to the Lord, "Lord, I cannot bear any more;" yet I had no fear of death.

How long I continued in this state, with this baptism continuing to roll over me and go through me, I do not know. But I know it was late in the evening when a member of my choir came into the office to see me. He was a member of the church. He found me in this state of loud weeping, and said to me, "Mr. Finney, what ails you?" I could make him no answer for some time. He then said, "Are you in pain?" I gathered up myself as best I could and replied, "No; but I am so happy that I cannot live."

For some, when God becomes real it is an amazing experience; I have many friends who have had astonishing experiences with God. For most of us, it is like Peter — an inner revelation that "you are the Christ, the Son of the living God" (Matthew 16:16). And later on they may have powerful experiences. We don't want to compare these experiences, but God wants to invade our world in a very profound way. Some more dramatic, some less, but an invasion just the same.

Remember, the Christian life is a powerful encounter with God on the inside that changes our spiritual DNA. We now don't just live for God because we are supposed to — we now live for God because there is a powerful force inside of us moving us in a divine direction. This has been my experience. It's like I enter in to a powerful river, and I am being moved by a powerful current.

Several years ago, my wife began to pray for me because I was becoming more of an intellectual Christian. The reality of His presence in my life was low. She had fallen head over heels in love with Jesus, and I was cold. She prayed very hard for me, and on an Easter Sunday something amazing happened to me. I began to cry and could not stop for three days. I did not know what was happening to me, but I knew it had to do with the love of God being poured out into my heart. At the end of these three days, I had fallen in love with Jesus. He had poured His love into my heart; my relationship was now based on a deep love for Him. This experience changed my whole Christian life; this intense love of God became the theme of my life. After that experience, I would spend time with Jesus because I was in love — not out of duty. I wanted to be with Him because I loved Him. God's love simply came and changed the direction of my life. This experience was an answer to my wife's prayers. Remember, the way forward is by asking.

My heart and prayer is, "God, make Yourself real to my friends and my family." This is why our first prayer priority is, "Your kingdom come on earth as it is in heaven."

I know the more real God becomes to me, the "deeper I can go with Him," the greater I can experience Him. This is the greatest thing that can happen to a human being. There is a greater world waiting for us to experience now today, this moment. We must ***ask for it. It is the eternal world that is far superior to this realm.***

This book has been about encountering God – praying for that encounter to happen in our lives. This is what the Lord's Prayer is about, asking God to become real. The Bible is a book about encounters with God. These encounters have not stopped with the New Testament, but are accelerating as we come closer to the end of the age.

Jesus taught us that asking is the way forward. How much more does your heavenly Father want to give the Holy Spirit to those who ask and keep on asking. Let this asking be our main priority (Luke 11:13).

Right after the Lord's Prayer in Luke 11:4, Jesus gave a parable. The following parable is a big key for us moving forward. Let's read it together from Luke 11:5-10:

> *"And He said to them, Which of you who has a friend will go to him at midnight and will say to him, Friend, lend me three loaves [of bread],*

"For a friend of mine who is on a journey has just come, and I have nothing to put before him;

"And he from within will answer, Do not disturb me; the door is now closed, and my children are with me in bed; I cannot get up and supply you [with anything]?

"I tell you, although he will not get up and supply him anything because he is his friend, yet because of his shameless persistence and insistence he will get up and give him as much as he needs.

"So I say to you, Ask and keep on asking and it shall be given you; seek and keep on seeking and you shall find; knock and keep on knocking and the door shall be opened to you.

"For everyone who asks and keeps on asking receives; and he who seeks and keeps on seeking finds; and to him who knocks and keeps on knocking, the door shall be opened."

It is interesting that in Luke this parable comes right after the Lord's Prayer. This parable gives us a great key. It describes the posture we must have in order to receive His kingdom in our lives – the posture we need to have for the presence of God to invade us. The posture is found in verse 8 – "shameless persistence and insistence." God loves for us to be bold and persistent with Him, because it shows our desire for Him and our love for Him. Shameless persistence shows desire. His desire for us took Him to the cross, so He loves for us to desire Him.

Remember, it is God who produces this desire in us. We can't "work it up," so we ask Him to produce this desire in us. He loves for us to pray that prayer and this prayer He will answer because His desire is for us to pursue Him because we love Him.

The friend in the parable would not take "no" for an answer, so Christ is saying, be this kind of person with Me. I love it!

To receive things in this life, many times it takes an uncompromising boldness, and so it is with God. To enter into His world and His realm, many times it takes an uncompromising boldness. God has so much of Himself that He wants to give us. Let's lay down the gauntlet and say, "This is what I want. I want to love You the same way You love me. God, I need passion and desire for You. "Remember, it is God who gives us the desire to know Him. Flesh and blood will not give us this desire. So the way forward is to ask. "God, draw me to You that I may run after You."

WHAT HAVE WE LEARNED FROM THIS CHAPTER?

1. God is not real to many Christians. He is just a world-view.

2. The Holy Spirit makes God real to us (John 16:14).

3. The Holy Spirit made Christ real to Peter and the early Christians in the upper room (Acts, chapter 2).

4. People want to live in the world that is real to them. The more real God becomes to me, the deeper I can go into Him.

5. The way for God to become real to us is to ask God for it. He so wants to be real to us. Jesus' prayer in John 17 was that we might see His glory. When we see His glory, He becomes real, like the disciples on the Mount of Transfiguration (Matthew 17:1-8).

6. Our prayers must be shameless and persistent and insistent. In Luke's gospel, right after the Lord's Prayer, Jesus teaches us a parable called "the friend at midnight." This parable is the key to our attitude. God loves for us to be shameless, persistent, and insistent. It reveals to Him that we really want Him because He really wants us to be persistent. Because He loves us.

7. The changes in our relationship with God cannot be a product of our will. It must come from an inner transformation like when Isaiah the prophet saw the Lord high and lifted up. He became completely undone. I will include this encounter at the end of this chapter. This encounter changed everything for Isaiah. God wants to encounter us in a way that we are completely undone. When God becomes real, everything changes. Our number one prayer needs to be, "God, become real to me."

PRAYER

God, make Yourself real to me that I may pursue You with all of my heart. You are the only eternal thing I have. Everything else will end in disappointment. Put into me a reality of You that gives me a desperation like the friend at midnight. I want Your love to draw me into oneness with You. Open my eyes. I want to see more clearly. I so want You closer, and You want a greater closeness with me. Holy Spirit, fall upon me. Make this happen inside me. Flesh and blood can't go there, but Your Spirit can take me there.

I would like to include the prophet Isaiah's encounter with God. This encounter Isaiah had is the moment God became real to him. It is found in Isaiah 6:1-8 NIV.

1 In the year that King Uzziah died, I saw the Lord, high and exalted, seated on a throne; and the train of his robe filled the temple.

2 Above him were seraphim, each with six wings: With two wings they covered their faces, with two they covered their feet, and with two they were flying.

3 And they were calling to one another:

> *"Holy, holy, holy is the Lord Almighty;*
> *the whole earth is full of his glory."*

4 At the sound of their voices the doorposts and thresholds shook and the temple was filled with smoke.

5 "Woe to me!" I cried. "I am ruined! For I am a man of unclean lips, and I live among a people of unclean lips, and my eyes have seen the King, the Lord Almighty."

6 Then one of the seraphim flew to me with a live coal in his hand, which he had taken with tongs from the altar. 7 With it he touched my mouth and said, "See, this has touched your lips; your guilt is taken away and your sin atoned for."

8 Then I heard the voice of the Lord saying, "Whom shall I send? And who will go for us?"

And I said, "Here am I. Send me!"

It is the intimate encounters we have with the living God that radically changes our lives. Most of these encounters are very calm and beautiful, but still they are encounters with the living God and every encounter large or small is amazing and life-changing. As with Isaiah, these encounters can ruin us in a wonderful way and change the course of our lives.

HEAVEN IS A PLACE OF EXTREME LOVE
FOR GOD AND EXTREME DEVOTION
TO HIM. HEAVEN IS 100 PERCENT
COMMITTED TO A DEEP
RELATIONSHIP WITH THE TRINITY,
AND LOVE IS THE ONLY MOTIVE.

CHAPTER 17

WHY LOVE GOD WITH ALL OUR HEART

Heaven is a place of extreme love for God and extreme devotion to Him. Heaven is 100 percent committed to a deep relationship with the Trinity, and love is the only motive.

Many people today ask the questions, "Why do we need to give all of ourself to God? Why do we need to love Him with all of our heart?" We live in an age of half commitments, self-centered love, and hedonism. The "I must be first" priority: "If I don't put myself first, no one else will look after me. Besides, life is about having fun and pursuing my own ambitions and dreams."

So, for Jesus to say that the greatest commandment is to love God with all your heart, all your soul, and all your mind, how does that fit into our present understanding? Because our relationship with God is based on love, it can be puzzling at the least. To understand this, we have to view this from God's perspective, not man's perspective.

God's love is huge. The Bible says in 1 John 4:7-8 that "God is love." When God came to earth in the second person of the Trinity, Jesus, the Bible tells us that the image of God was clearly seen. So why did He come, and what was His mission?

Jesus came to love us with everything that was in Him. He was in 100 percent. Love was His overwhelming motive. John 3:16 NKJV says, *"For God so loved the world...."* A look at Scripture and you see that God's intense love for us was His only motive for sending Jesus. It was not a timid or cold love or a small love. It was an all out love, a passionate love.

There are so many Scriptures describing God's intense love that I can't put them all in this chapter. I will list them at the end of this chapter. First John 3:1 says, *"See what [an incredible] quality of love the Father has given (shown, bestowed on) us, that we should [be permitted to] be named and called and counted the children of God...."*

Ephesians 2:4-5 says:

"But God – so rich is He in His mercy! Because of and in order to satisfy the great and wonderful and intense love with which He loved us,

"Even when we were dead (slain) by [our own] shortcomings and trespasses, He made us alive together in fellowship and in union with Christ; [He gave us the very life of Christ Himself...."

It would be good to read the rest of Ephesians 2. These verses keep building as they continue with absolutely amazing words. (As I mentioned, I will list these verses at the end of this chapter. It would help to read them in their entirety.)

The one thing we must grasp is God's great, overwhelming love for us. This is not a passive love. This love is looking for a response from the one it loves. The verse we just read says that God has something in Him that needs to be satisfied. He is in love with us and wants our love and companionship. This is what satisfies the heart of God.

When the apostle Paul was writing about marriage, he paused in the middle of a sentence and said:

"For this reason a man shall leave his father and his mother and shall be joined to his wife, and the two shall become one flesh.

"This mystery is very great, but I speak concerning [the relation of] Christ and the church."

Ephesians 5:31-32

So Paul is comparing our relationship to Christ to a marriage. It is greater than an earthly marriage, but, it contains the same principles as a marriage. A great love on the part of one requires a response from the other. The desire of marital love leads two to become one, but both must desire to be with the other. Both must commit to being one, and the desire to be together becomes the force driving them.

They become willing to give up all other lovers, move to the same location, give up friends, jobs, whatever it takes to be together. Some give up country, family fortunes, and crowns just to be together. They must overcome all obstacles because being together is the driving force.

This is our analogy when it comes to the love God has for us. God is willing to clear all obstacles to be one with us. Jesus did not come just so our sins can be forgiven. He died and took upon Himself our sins so we could be one with Him, dwell with Him and He with us. It took something drastic, something awful, in order for us to be one with Him.

Jesus said in John 6:56, *"He who feeds on My flesh and drinks My blood dwells continually in Me, and I [in like manner dwell continually] in him."* This verse may sound strange, but this is the level of oneness God's love is striving for. This is God's desire: that we actually take Jesus into us, and He lives inside of us and we dwell inside of Him. There is no other level of closeness than this. This is the ultimate of oneness. Because He is God, He can dwell inside of us, fusing His Spirit with ours.

First Corinthians 6:17 says, *"But the person who is united to the Lord becomes one spirit with Him."* This level of oneness can only be achieved when both parties are 100 percent committed to the relationship. The Bible is very clear that Jesus' commitment to us is total, so where does that leave us?

Jesus made a statement in Matthew 10:37-38 that is very telling:

"He who loves [and takes more pleasure in] father or mother more than [in] Me is not worthy of Me; and he

who loves [and takes more pleasure in] son or daughter more than [in] Me is not worthy of Me;

"And he who does not take up his cross and follow Me [cleave steadfastly to Me, conforming wholly to My example in living and, if need be, in dying also] is not worthy of Me."

God's love for us is 100 percent. Here Jesus is addressing our love for Him. If we love someone or anything greater than our love for Him, He says we are not worthy of Him. Remember, our relationship with God is a spiritual marriage.

The word "worthy" may throw us off. It would be like a loving, giving, sweet girl who is going to marry an egotistical guy who is selfish and only in love with himself. We would say this is a mismatch. He is not worthy of her.

Here Jesus is addressing a mismatch. He is saying, "I love you completely, but you love someone or something else more than Me. There is something you love more, and it is preventing us from being one."

These verses do not say we are not to love our parents or others. The second commandment says, *"Love your neighbor as you do yourself."* When we love God supremely over all other loves, our love for others increases because of the union He now has with us. His love floods our hearts and flows out to others.

Because God's passion is to be one with us, things get real serious. We are talking about God's love. Some may say, "I wish You did not love me so much," but we can't avoid it. We must deal with it and be glad that He does love us so much.

So our response must be to love Him back supremely. Put all other loves in their proper place. Commit to 100 percent devotion to God, and something amazing will happen.

Union with God on a level we would never think possible will produce a love inside of us that will blow our minds. If it is based on great love, it won't be hard. Let's ask God to pour out His love in our hearts. *"Such hope never disappoints or deludes or shames us, for God's love has been poured out in our hearts through the Holy Spirit Who has been given to us"* (Romans 5:5). This great love He has for us will propel us forward.

Oh God, pour Your love into my heart and draw me to You that I may love You back with the same intensity with which You love me. You have sent your Holy Spirit to me, to make this miracle possible.

WHAT HAVE WE LEARNED FROM THIS CHAPTER?

1. Heaven is a place of extreme love for God. Heaven is 100 percent committed to a deep relationship with the Trinity. God has a 100 percent commitment to love the inhabitants of heaven. He cares for them and will wipe away all their tears.

2. The greatest commandment is to love the Lord your God with 100 percent of your heart, 100 percent of your soul, 100 percent of your mind, and 100 percent of your strength. If it is a commandment, then God will give us the grace (supernatural strength) to do it (Matthew 22:37; Luke 10:27; Deuteronomy 6:5).

3. Jesus came to earth to love us with everything in Him. The cross shows us this love. Jesus was 100 percent committed to love us (John 15:9).

4. Jesus came to earth to fulfill and satisfy the intense love He has for us.

5. Ephesians 2:4 says: *"But God—so rich is He in His mercy! Because of and in order to satisfy the great and wonderful and intense love with which He loved us."*

6. Paul said our relationship with Christ is like a marriage. It is greater than an earthly marriage, but it operates on the same principles. The great love on the part of one requires a great response from the other. Both must desire to be one and be together in the same location (Ephesians 5:31-32).

7. Jesus did not come just to forgive our sins. He came so we could be one with Him (1 Corinthians 6:17).

8. God's desire is for us to take Jesus inside of us permanently into every cell of our body (John 6:56).

9. Jesus said if we love anything more than Him, we are not worthy of Him. The word "worthy" means our relationship is a mismatch. It means He loves us more than we love Him (Matthew 10:37-38).

10. If we put God in first place and love Him with all our hearts, something amazing will happen (Matthew 6:33).

This is not impossible. God has given us the ability by His Holy Spirit for this to happen. It is supernatural.

11. As we stare at the crucified Christ, it speaks to us of Jesus' passionate love for us – a love with no compromise. This is the level we must rise to. We can't leave Him alone on the cross. We must embrace His love. The cross is saying, "I won't compromise. I want to be one with you" (John 15:9). Will you be one with Me?

12. There is a beautiful Scripture in Jeremiah 29:12-13: *"Then you will call upon Me, and you will come and pray to Me, and I will hear and heed you. Then you will seek Me, inquire for, and require Me [as a vital necessity] and find Me when you search for Me with all your heart."*

13. It takes the presence and power of God to accomplish this in us. Don't get discouraged. Pray for God to do those things in your heart. Remember, prayer is the way forward.

PRAYER

God, I ask for Your power to enable me to love You with everything in me. My mind can be so divided. Let me see Your glory. Become more real to me than the world around me. You are the only eternal Being. Invade my life and make me like You! I want to love You with the same intensity You love me. This love can only be supernatural, so I am boldly asking You for it. Pour out Your love into my heart.

Further Study:

Look at these Scriptures on God's intense love for us. This should leave no doubt how God feels about us.

Ephesians 3:18-19
Psalm 5:11-12
1 John 3:1
Ephesians 1:5
John 3:16
Romans 5:8
Ephesians 2:4-5
2 Corinthians 5:14-15
Romans 5:5
Proverbs 3:11-12
Psalm 31:7
Lamentations 3:20-23
Lamentations 3:32-33
John 13:3-5, 34
1 John 4:9-12

Note: A relationship with God is not the kind of relationship where He just gives us things or answers our wants; although, He does do that. What Jesus wants is to give us Himself in a relationship and wants us to give ourselves to Him. Material things are not God's main priority. His priority is companionship.

"FATHER, I DESIRE THAT THEY ALSO WHOM YOU HAVE ENTRUSTED TO ME [AS YOUR GIFT TO ME] MAY BE WITH ME WHERE I AM, SO THAT THEY MAY SEE MY GLORY..."
(JOHN 17:24).

THIS PRAYER IS JESUS' GREATEST DESIRE. REALIZING THAT THIS IS THE CENTRAL THEME OF THE BIBLE, THE CENTER OF JESUS' HEART, WILL HELP US INTERPRET THE MAIN THEME OF REDEMPTION AND THE CENTRAL THEME OF THE BIBLE.

CHAPTER **18**

HEAVEN IS NOT LUKEWARM

As we have discussed before, God is speaking to us from heaven. God loves to speak to us because He loves us. Speaking to one another is an act of love. People who are married and don't speak to each other soon fall out of love. Through conversation, we become intimate with one another. When our deepest thoughts are exposed, closeness is the result. It is the same way in our relationship with God.

Jesus, in Scripture, exposes His deepest longings with us, and we learn to expose our deepest longings with Him. God is not just a doctrine or rules or a Bible. He is a real being with desires and longings toward us, His creation. Learning about God is not the same as experiencing God. This is the problem with long-distance relationships. They don't feel real or intimate. God wants to be close to us, so close He wants to come inside us and wants us to come inside Him. He wants this because He is in love with us.

In the book of Revelation (Revelation 2 and 3), Jesus sends letters to seven churches. These letters are full of encouragement, but also correction. In the book of Hebrews, chapter 12, verse 6, it says, *"For the Lord corrects and disciplines everyone whom He loves, and He punishes, even scourges, every son whom He accepts and welcomes to His heart and cherishes."* So we must see correction as love, intense love.

Read the letter to the church at Laodicea before we continue in this chapter. It will help you understand the context. Read Revelation 3:14-22.

Jesus tells them they are neither hot nor cold but lukewarm. Then He says something scary: *"I will spew you out of My mouth"* (v. 16). That is strong talk. Intense love speaks truth and shares how it feels about a situation. We must remember that this is love talking; this is a groom talking to His bride. Sharing His heart with her, sharing His pain. Jesus was experiencing pain, because His love was not being returned.

Jesus wants us to be hot. The illustration of being hot denotes passion, fervency. The dictionary defines "lukewarm" as lacking conviction or enthusiasm, indifferent, or neutral. Remember, Jesus wants us to be hot because of His intense love for us.

The other night, I was talking to a young man who had some hard decisions to make. As we talked, we used the illustration of hot, lukewarm, and cold. For your hot to become lukewarm, you mix the hot water with the cold water. So we talked about his decisions. This young man is hot when it comes to God, so we looked at each decision as hot or cold.

One decision was a beautiful girl he knew was a compromised Christian, so we looked at this situation and decided that it was cold. If I incorporate her into my hot world, I will bring down the temperature, maybe even to lukewarm.

Another decision was an opportunity to play music in a popular band. We looked at it as hot or cold. He said that opportunity was definitely cold, so he based his decision on what would lead to lukewarmness.

We then looked at some other opportunities that looked hot. These would fuel his passion to love God more, so he decided to go in that direction.

I am using this as an illustration. I know every decision is not that simple. With decisions, we need to be led by the Spirit of God and hear God's voice. But sometimes it is very obvious what will lead us to a lukewarm relationship with Jesus. Sometimes we talk ourselves out of the obvious, knowing it will lead us to lukewarmness. Sometimes we make excuses like, "There is nothing wrong with this." In reality, we know where it will lead us.

Whether something is morally right or wrong should not be how we evaluate major decisions. Because that is not the goal. The goal is a very close, tight relationship with God. So our decisions should be based on that. Does this decision lead me to being closer to Jesus, or does it put distance between us? Like in a marriage, our decision should be, does this help our relationship, or does it damage our relationship; many people don't use this to evaluate their decisions, and it can lead to divorce or distancing of the relationship. Closeness with God is the standard by which we should judge life.

God will help us if we will be honest with Him and if we will discuss these things with Him. He wants conversation with us. We are invited into the very throne room of God to discuss our situations with the Father, the Son, and the Holy Spirit. God will send supernatural help to strengthen us in our decisions.

Jesus wants us to be hot. Loving Him with all our hearts, all our soul, all our mind, and all our strength (Mark 12:30), no longer living to just please ourself, but living to please Him. He lives for us, so we need to live for Him. Remember, we are in a spiritual marriage. Heaven would be considered very hot. Hot is passionate love for God; cold is indifference to Him.

In the letter written by Jesus to the church in Laodicea, He said in Revelation 3, verse 17, *"For you say, I am rich; I have prospered and grown wealthy, and I am in need of nothing...."* But in reality, Jesus saw them differently *"you do not realize and understand that you are wretched, pitiable, poor, blind, and naked."*

It's amazing that you could see yourself as rich and in need of nothing, and God could see you as wretched, pitiable, poor, blind, and naked. That is so scary. It shows how far self-deception can take a person.

Jesus then says, *"Therefore I counsel you to purchase from Me gold refined and tested by fire, that you may be [truly] wealthy, and white clothes to clothe you and to keep the shame of your nudity from being seen, and salve to put on your eyes, that you may see"* (Revelation 3:18).

Then He says, *"So be enthusiastic and in earnest and burning with zeal and repent [changing your mind and attitude]"* (v. 19).

In Revelation 3:20 we see the solution to lukewarmness: *"Behold, I stand at the door and knock; if anyone hears and listens to and heeds My voice and opens the door, I will come in to him and will eat with him, and he [will eat] with Me."*

As we have studied, God's number one desire is to be with us, talk with us, fellowship with us, and be in union with us. Because God is love (1 John 4:8 and 1 John 4:16). As we have said, before the last prayer Jesus prayed, right before He was betrayed, in John 17:24 He said:

> *"Father, I desire that they also whom You have entrusted to Me [as Your gift to Me] may be with Me where I am, so that they may see My glory...."*

This prayer is Jesus' greatest desire. Realizing that this is the central theme of the Bible, the center of Jesus' heart, will help us to interpret the main theme of redemption, the center theme of the Bible. Jesus' desire for the lukewarm church is, "Open your heart to Me that we may fellowship together. That we might deeply love each other and spend time together."

"Behold, I stand at the door and knock. Open the door and fellowship with Me." This is Jesus' ultimate desire. Money, goods, houses, cars, and comfort — all of this is secondary to fellowship with Jesus. If we step back and look at this, it is mind-blowing. We can have deep, intimate fellowship — as

deep as we want to go with the God who created a universe, 93 billion light years across with 100 billion galaxies, each galaxy containing 100,000,000,000 stars. The God who created this fabulous universe wants to get small enough to fit in your heart and have fellowship with you! For me, I don't want to miss this. It's too amazing and so significant.

This letter to the church at Laodicea ends with an amazing invitation from Jesus: "I will invite everyone who is victorious and overcomes to sit with Me on My throne." (See Revelation 3:20.) Many translations say, "Sit beside Me on My throne."

Just as I myself have won the victory and have taken my seat beside my Father on His throne, I am going out on a limb with this verse. There are a lot of opinions as to what this means. I will leave you with an idea. Jesus' number one desire is for us to be with Him where He is. If we defeat lukewarmness, and I believe this is our biggest battle, we will find ourselves fellowshipping with Christ, sitting next to Him in the throne room of heaven, the center of the universe.

Lately, as I pray, I see myself in the throne room talking to the Trinity. The Father is there listening and talking. The Son (Jesus) is there listening and talking and loving me, and the Holy Spirit is there listening and talking.

Let's not see this as a future event, but as an invitation to the present (now). If we are lukewarm, we won't even hear the invitation or see Him high and lifted up. There are Scriptures that tell us we are welcome in the throne room of God. Hebrews 4:14-16 in the *New Living Translation* says,

"That is why we have a great High Priest who has gone to heaven, Jesus the Son of God let us cling to Him and never stop trusting Him.

"This High Priest of ours understands our weakness, for He faced all of the same temptations we do, yet He did not sin.

"So let us come boldly to the throne of our gracious God. There we will receive His mercy, and we will find grace to help us when we need it."

That is amazing — we can go into the throne room of God where we will find Jesus, our High Priest, who understands our weaknesses, who is gracious to us. We will find mercy, grace, and power to help us in our need. You can't find that anywhere in this world. This is where we need to spend time every day. There is emotional healing in the throne room of God.

The throne room of God is the one place in all the universe we need to go and hang out. There is tremendous power there – power we need on earth. As we go there and spend time, we bring back to earth the things we need here: power, healing, love, mercy, and grace.

Thy will be done on earth as it is in heaven.

WHAT HAVE WE LEARNED IN THIS CHAPTER?

1. God is in love with us, so love is the measure of all things relating to God.

2. God wants us to talk deeply with Him. Conversation leads to intimacy. God wants us to pour our hearts out to Him, and He wants to pour His heart out to us.

3. Jesus said, "I have loved you as much as the Father has loved Me." (See John 15:9.) That is all out love – intense love. God wants us to love Him back like that.

4. Being lukewarm toward God is a very bad thing. Like a wife who is lukewarm toward her husband – that leaves her vulnerable to other men.

5. Because of the blood of Jesus, we can go right into the throne room of God and talk intimately with Him. This is where we get our strength (Hebrews 4:14).

6. We can't overcome lukewarmness on our own. It's the power of God given to us because of the blood that was poured out for us. We must depend on Him from start to finish (Hebrews 4:14). Let us cling to Him.

7. To run with Christ, our nature must change. We must be like Him. God has made this possible. We can be born again. John 3:3 NIV says, *"Very truly I tell you, no one can see the kingdom of God unless they are born again."* We have been given the ability to see God by being born anew — being born into His realm. So let's go for it!!!

PRAYER

Jesus, pour Your love into my heart so I may love You back with great intensity. This is the direction I want my life to go in. Accomplish in me what is impossible for me to do. I don't want to be lukewarm. Rescue me. Be my Deliverer. Flood me with Your presence so I can run after You. You are the only thing of ultimate value to me. Come to me. Bring Your intimacy so that we can be one.

GOD'S LOVE FOR US IS INTENSELY

GREAT. THE NATURE OF LOVE

IS TO BE WITH THOSE YOU LOVE.

CHAPTER 19

THE GREATEST OF ALL INVITATIONS

As we have discussed before, God's love for us is intensely great. Jesus prayed in John 17:24, "My desire is those You have given Me would be with Me where I am." The nature of love is to be with those you love. This is the theme of the whole Bible.

A bride and groom buy a house or rent an apartment. Their greatest desire is to be together. When I got married, my wife did not care how much money I would make or my career or where we would live. She just wanted to be with me.

We bought a trailer. She loved that trailer because there we could be together. I am so thankful that love for me was her reason for her marriage to me – not what I could provide. I was at the university studying. We had no money and sometimes very little to eat, but we were together. That's all that mattered.

We did not feel poor because we had each other. We had our struggles, but the love we had for each other got us through.

Jesus desires that kind of relationship. He wants to be with us, not just on a theological level or have Him as our world-view or a belief system. He wants to come into us in a greater way and be one with us and have deep conversations with us. He wants to make His home inside of us. He does not want to live in buildings; He wants to live in us.

All through Scripture, Jesus is inviting mankind to come and live with Him and in Him. Again, we must not see this as a future event. God's love for us is so great He wants to live in us now. He does not want to wait for a future date. He desires us <u>now</u>.

The invitations of Jesus are astounding. He was constantly giving invitations to come to Him because there is a massive amount of love flowing out of Him; and love can only be satisfied by being with the one you love.

On the last day of the Feast, Jesus stood up and He cried in a loud voice, *"If any man is thirsty, let him <u>come to Me</u> and drink"* (John 7:37). This was coming from His heart. It was so strong He just stood up and yelled it out. He could not keep from saying it. It was like a groom yelling to his bride, "I love you and want to spend the rest of my life with you."

Jesus was constantly giving passionate invitations. When He met His disciples, He cried, "Come and follow Me" (Matthew 4:19). He cried out to Zacchaeus who climbed up a tree so he could get a better look at Jesus. Jesus looked up with love and said to Zacchaeus, *"Hurry and come down; for I must stay at your house today."* Jesus said, "I must." This was love talking (Luke 19:1-10). I *must* be with you today.

Jesus is saying that to us: "Hurry and come down. I must stay at your house today." I *must* be with you today.

The invitation in John 15:3-4 is astounding. Jesus invites us to dwell in Him, and He says, *"Dwell in Me, and I will dwell in you..."* (v. 4). In other words, "I will make My home in you." That is what "dwell" means. He says, "You won't bear fruit unless you live (make your home) in Me." Read John, chapter 15. It is astounding.

Jesus was constantly giving invitations to come to Him. They were intense invitations like, "Come, live in Me (make Me your home)." This is not just "Believe in Jesus." This is "Change your address. Make Me your home. Hire a mover and move into Me."

Jesus gave an invitation to a rich young ruler. *"And Jesus, looking upon him, loved him, and He said to him, You lack one thing; go and sell all you have and give [the money] to the poor and come follow me..."* (Mark 10:21). The rich young ruler became grieved, gloomy, and sorrowful. He realized to answer the invitation Jesus was giving him, he would have to give up his other loves. Following Jesus is intense love!

Our relationship to Jesus is a marriage, so we can't have competing lovers. In Matthew 11:28 Jesus says, *"Come to Me, all you who labor and are heavy-laden and overburdened, and I will cause you to rest. [I will ease and relieve and refresh your souls.]"*

These invitations from Jesus are all about coming to Him one on one — nothing in between, just Him. Coming directly to Him and making Him our <u>home</u>. I can't express this strongly enough – nothing else, just Him.

Jesus, throughout His ministry, was giving invitations to come to Him, beginning with the parable of a wedding feast where the guests had other more important things to do (Luke 14:15-24).

Verses 18-23 say:

"But they all alike began to make excuses and to beg off. The first said to him, I have bought a piece of land, and I have to go out and see it; I beg you, have me excused.

"And another said, I have bought five yoke of oxen, and I am going to examine and put my approval on them; I beg you, have me excused.

"And another said, I have married a wife, and because of this I am unable to come.

"So the servant came and reported these [answers] to his master. Then the master of the house said in wrath to his servant, Go quickly into the great streets and the small streets of the city and bring in here the poor and the disabled and the blind and the lame.

"And the servant [returning] said, Sir, what you have commanded me to do has been done, and yet there is room.

"Then the master said to the servant, Go out into the highways and hedges and urge and constrain [them] to yield and come in, so that my house may be filled."

Jesus was constantly inviting people to come to Him. His motive was love, and what He gave them was Himself, which is eternal life.

Lord, help us to see. Give us eyes to see what Your invitation means – how much greater your invitation is. It is far above anything else.

At the very end of the book of Revelation, there is an invitation that we give for people to come to Jesus. In Revelation 22:17, it says, *"The [Holy] Spirit and the bride (the church, the true Christians) say, Come! And let him who is listening say, Come! And let everyone come who is thirsty [who is painfully conscious of his need of those things by which the soul is refreshed, supported, and strengthened]; and whoever [earnestly] desires to do it, let him come, take, appropriate, and drink the water of Life without cost."*

We remember from the last chapter that Jesus says, *"To him who overcomes I will grant to sit with Me on My throne, as I also overcame and sat down with My Father on His throne"* (Revelation 3:21 NKJV).

All through Jesus' time here on earth, He was giving invitations. There are so many we can't mention them all in this chapter, but His life was one big invitation to come to Him.

With all invitations, there are things we must do. An invitation is permission to go somewhere. Usually we dress up and arrive at a location at a certain time. Only certain people are invited, so sometimes we feel kind of special. To answer an invitation we must rearrange our schedule, hire a baby sitter, buy new clothes, put gas in the car, and travel a distance. Sometimes it takes great effort, but it is worth the reward. Going to the event is very rewarding.

Jesus is giving us an invitation to come to Him, and it is for everyone. So stop what you are doing and go. This invitation is the greatest of all invitations; to ignore this one would be tragic.

Let's end this chapter where we started — with the Lord's Prayer. The first thing we are to pray in the Lord's Prayer is, "Your kingdom come." This is our invitation for Jesus to come. Oh, how He loves to be invited. It's the number one desire in God's heart. When we pray that prayer, a completely different world opens up to us. This is what the heart of Jesus wants. He wants to be invited.

WHAT HAVE WE LEARNED FROM THIS CHAPTER?

1. Jesus' whole life was one big invitation to come unto Him. Jesus was constantly inviting people to come to Him.

2. The nature of love is to be with the ones you love. Jesus' love for us is massive.

3. Jesus wants us to be with Him, to actually be one with Him.

4. Jesus loves it when we return the invitation and invite Him to come into us. One of these invitations is found in Revelation 22:17.

5. The first thing we are to pray for in the Lord's Prayer is, "Your kingdom come." It is our invitation for Him to come.

6. A home is where we live and dwell. It is shelter, comfort, a warm place, safety, enjoyment, a place of peace and solitude. Jesus becomes our home and we became His home. Remember, it's not just about how we feel; God has feelings also, and His desire is that we become His home — a place He can enter where there is warmth and love. When Jesus was on earth, He was homeless; this tells us He was looking for a home, and that home is you and me. In Revelations, He was standing outside knocking, wanting to come in. Jesus said, "If anyone hears my voice and opens the door, I will come in to Him" (Revelation 3:20). This is the desire of Jesus. We are His home, and He is wanting to come in and live.

PRAYER

Jesus, You are the fountain of all I am looking for. Everything else is a well that will run dry. Pour Your love on me so that I can love You back without reserve. I do love You. Increase my love by revealing Your love for me. Come make Your home inside of me. I want to make a home for You there. Open my eyes so I can see Your desire for me.

MUCH OF THE BIBLE IS GOD DOING
SUPERNATURAL THINGS, THEN PEOPLE
RECORDING WHAT GOD DID.

CHAPTER **20**

WHEN STRANGE THINGS HAPPEN

I have been in youth ministry for many years, working in public schools, starting Christian clubs, talking to youth at lunch, doing camps, and from time to time, amazing things would happen – things that defy comprehension —events that just made me stand back in amazement. Sometimes it seemed that heaven just opened up and its contents are spilled onto the earth.

Like John on the Isle of Patmos, "[He] was in the Spirit [rapt in His power] on the Lord's Day" (Revelation 1:10). Heaven just descended, on him unexpectedly, and he fell at the feet of Jesus as if he were dead.

Paul was on a mission to persecute the church, and God unexpectedly descended on him, knocking him to the ground and blinding him. Acts 9:1-19, Acts 22:6-21, and Acts 26:12-18, take time to read these verses; it will help give us some understanding. This encounter Paul had with Jesus is so important it is told three times in the Book of Acts. This one encounter was a pivotal event in early Christianity. Without this encounter, things would have been vastly different.

Jesus took Peter, James, and John to the Mount of Transfiguration where Jesus' appearance underwent a supernatural change. His face shone bright like the sun, and His clothing became as white as light. A shiny cloud overshadowed them, and a voice spoke from the cloud. They fell on their faces in terror. (Matthew 17:1-9)

As we have said before, much of the Bible is God doing supernatural things; then people recording what God did. Like Mary, the mother of Jesus, as supernatural things began to happen all around her, all she could do was: *"But Mary treasured up all these things and pondered them in her heart"* (Luke 2:19 NIV).

One such event took place on a trip to a series of meetings in Florida. We had about thirty youth with us. These were normal teenagers. Some just wanted to go to Florida. We attended a series of meetings, but I was not sure what had happened to them. They seemed to have a good time, and God seemed to be working in their lives.

On the way home, we were in two 15-passenger vans. The teens in the van behind us started to argue with each other as teens sometimes do. One of the teens got upset and said,

"If we go home with this attitude, we will lose everything we have gotten from this week." So they decided to pray and ask for forgiveness. As each prayed, something amazing started to happen. The presence of heaven descended upon them. They began to weep loudly.

We got off the highway and pulled up to a Citgo gas station in Clarksville, Arkansas. When we stopped, the teens in the van who were crying rushed up to the van in front, opened the doors, and began praying for the teens in the front van. What happened frightened me. They all got out of the van, and many fell to the pavement like they were dead. I stood over them, making sure no one got run over. Some were crying while others were lying like they were dead. Remember, these were teenagers, and many just wanted to go to Florida.

Someone called the police. When the police arrived, I ran to his car to explain what had happened. He was not happy. He went into the station to talk to the owner. The owner told him to leave them alone, that what was happening was from the "Big Man upstairs." That is how he described God.

So there we were at a gas station in Clarksville, Arkansas, with thirty teens, many lying on an oil-stained pavement like they were dead. People would pull up to the pump, but no one would get out. People could not figure out what was happening, and we were not quite sure ourselves what this meant. But I have read many books on great awakenings in America, England, and other parts of the world to know these things happen.

After a couple of hours, they came to and we all began to worship, dance, and pray. For many of these teens, this experience was when God became real. God was no longer a Bible verse or something their parents believed in. God was now real to them, and they would never be the same, and I would never be the same.

There were so many supernatural experiences that happened to us over the years. One incident happened after the Asbury Revival. A young man was greatly touched by the presence of God. He got a bunch of his friends to meet in a home so he could tell them what had happened to him. One group he was concerned with was the high school athletes he knew. They came and listened, but as soon as the meeting was over, they thought this was not for them and left. He was greatly disappointed.

They got in the car, and about a block away heaven opened up on them. They began to feel a strange sensation and began to cry. There was one student who had a Christian background and knew what was happening. He led them in a prayer. God entered their hearts, and when they returned to their high school, an amazing move of God's Spirit started to happen. Hundreds of students were affected. They had meetings where so many students came, they had to meet outside.

There were camps we had where when worship started, most of the teens would fall to the ground and begin crying and praying. We would stand back in amazement. Many of these teens are amazing Christians today.

I could tell stories of all-night prayer meetings and visions teens had. I feel like Mary who treasured up all these things and pondered them in her heart. There were so many lives permanently changed because heaven descended to earth. I feel so fortunate just to have been there and involved.

History repeats itself. In the future, we will see heaven and earth collide in amazing ways. Remember, the first thing we are to pray for is for God's will to be done on earth <u>exactly</u> as it is in heaven. There are things that will happen that will defy reason. So all we can pray is, *"Heaven, come, pour your contents on this earth. We desperately need you to become real to us and to those around us."* So many young people leave Christianity because God is not real to them. Our prayer is God become real to them.

WHAT HAVE WE LEARNED FROM THIS CHAPTER?

1. The Christian church started in the upper room. Jesus said in Luke 24:49 NLT, *"But stay here in the city until the Holy Spirit comes and fills you with power from heaven."* In the second chapter of Acts, the Holy Spirit descended on them and strange, supernatural things began to happen. The church started with an amazing supernatural event. (Acts, chapter 2.

2. As we have said in this book, much of the Bible is supernatural events happening, and the people recording what God had done.

3. A study of church history will tell us that God still comes in supernatural ways. Many denominations started from powerful outpourings from heaven. The Methodist church started from outpourings in John Wesley's meetings in England. Reading John Wesley's Journal is a real eye-opener. The Christian church (Disciples of Christ) started from the Cane Ridge Revival. The Baptist picked up the outpouring from Cane Ridge and spread it across the frontier. Studying the great awakenings in America and England can give us a new perspective of what it means when we pray, "Your will be done on earth as it is in heaven."

4. God has not stopped pouring out His Spirit upon mankind. He continues to do it today. For so many, God is a set of rules, ideas, and beliefs, but He is so much more. He is real and wants to pour heaven, His realm, onto us in astonishing ways. I don't want to labor this too much. The Holy Spirit is what makes God real to us. Without the Holy Spirit, Christianity is just a fantasy, hard to believe in. This is why the world around us is so opposed to the teachings of Christ. This is why people don't understand Christ (Colossians 3:1-3). Because He is not real to them.

PRAYER

God, come pour out Your contents on us. We know this world is not our permanent home. Come, make heaven real to me.

Read: *John Wesley's Journal, Volume 2,* pp. 472-477.

ETERNAL THINGS HAVE MUCH

GREATER POTENTIAL THAN

TEMPORAL THINGS.

CHAPTER 21

POTENTIAL

The other day, a friend of mine made a statement. He said, "Jesus is a choice, and Jesus is the weightiest of choices." As I began to think about what he was saying, I started to think about potential – about how much potential do the things I pursue have?

There are things in life that have very limited potential; others have great potential. The definition of "potential" is having the capacity to become or develop into something in the future.

During World War II, America was developing weapons to help win the war. Tanks, guns, airplanes, and submarines – but there was one weapon that had a greater potential than all others combined. A weapon with astronomical potential – the atomic bomb. If this weapon worked, it had the potential to stop the war in its tracks.

The scientist who was working on this weapon said that mass was energy and energy was mass, that inside everything we see, touch, and taste is a massive amount of energy, locked up inside atoms.

Albert Einstein came up with an amazing formula. Many of us know this formula. It was simple: $E=Mc^2$ or E is energy, M is mass, and C is the speed of light. If you multiply mass times the speed of light, it will tell you how much energy is locked up in mass. Mass is the stuff we see: rocks, trees, water, etc. He said that if you take the speed of light and multiply it by the speed of light that is how much energy is stored up in matter. Everything around us has massive energy stored up inside it. The tree in our front yard has enough energy stored up inside it to power your home for years, but it is locked up inside its atoms so we can't use it.

This is amazing – 186,000 miles per second, the speed of light, multiplied by 186,000 miles per second. That number is 90,000,000,000. That is the amount of energy in even the smallest mass. This is hard to comprehend, so what Einstein was saying was that there is an astronomical amount of energy pinned up in every atom. And if we could figure out how to release this energy, we could make a bomb greater than anything imaginable.

The scientist convinced the U. S. Government that this could work, so the United States invested hundreds of millions of dollars developing a bomb that was unimaginable. Many said it would not work, it was just a theoretical dream, but there was enough scientists convinced it would work to try it. America was desperate. To lose the war was unimaginable, so they threw all their resources into this project.

They built three whole cities from scratch to work on this project: Oak Ridge, Tennessee; Los Alamos, New Mexico; and Hanford/Richmond in Washington state. They hired 125,000 people to work on the project to build an atomic bomb. The people working on the project had no idea what they were working on.

Then on July 16, 1945, 210 miles south of Los Alamos, New Mexico, they tested the new device. The scientist who envisioned the bomb did not know if it would work. To their amazement, it worked — setting off an explosion that absolutely shocked everyone. It actually worked, and it was frightening.

To invade Japan it was estimated the United States would lose about 1 million soldiers and Japan would lose 10 million, so President Truman made a decision to use the bomb to end the war immediately. He dropped an atomic bomb on Hiroshima, Japan. He asked for an immediate surrender, but Japan said "no." So a second bomb was dropped on Nagasaki, Japan, and Japan surrendered immediately unconditionally. The atomic bomb the size of a car ended a massive war. War is a horrible thing, unbelievably horrible. I used this example from history, to show potential. I pray nothing this horrible ever happens again.

The reason that I was thinking about the atomic bomb was that everything we do has potential.

Another illustration would be a coal miner in Appalachia. He has a steady job working in a coal mine. His job has potential. He gets a paycheck each week, enough to buy food and live in a small house, but he will probably develop a lung disease and become disabled or die in a mine explosion. His job has potential. Then he finds out his brother who owns a gold mine in Arizona just died and left him his gold mine.

People had said his brother had found gold and was making a good living, so the coal miner had to make a decision: Do I keep my low potential job or move to something that has great potential?

The reason I have been thinking about this is because God has been speaking to me to go deeper with Him, and I am not sure exactly what that will require, so I began to look at potential. God was calling me deeper with Him. Another voice was telling me, "You're wasting your time."

So I began to think, "I am interacting with the God of the universe, and through Christ I can be as one with Him as I want." The formula is found in the words of Jesus. I began to look at what in my life has the greatest potential. It was obvious — a deep relationship with the God who created a billion galaxies and a billion things we don't even know about. Everything I do in my earthly life has limited potential because everything of material substance on this planet is dying.

My goal when I was in my early twenties was to be the world's greatest architect. I grew up with a very low self-esteem. My sister was a genius. I was not like my sister, so my mother thought I was mentally challenged. So I had to do something big to prove to everyone I was smart, talented, and incredible.

A year before I entered architectural school, Christ came into me. It was very mysterious. One night I had a dream. It was about all the great buildings I had created. They were magnificent. Then I saw a ball and crane knocking them down to make way for something better. Then I heard these words: "Where will you be in 10,000 years, and where will your buildings be in 10,000 years?" The value and potential of my career took a hit! I was not looking at things from a 30- or 40-year perspective, but looking farther into the future to find a greater worth, a greater potential.

Jesus had just entered into me and was giving me an eternal perspective. I saw that everything I had put my hopes in was temporal, and my career was actually to build up my sagging ego. I could never do enough to prop that up, because some people will like you and your work, others won't. There are plenty of critics in the world, so it's a never-ending cycle to try to get self-worth from what we do.

So my conclusion was, if Jesus was true and if the God of the universe has come on the inside of me, that has the greatest potential. It is not limited by time. I now have the very life of God living in me. Eternal life was living inside me, so I made a decision that Jesus would be my pursuit in life because He was the One with ultimate potential, staggering potential. I had discovered the nuclear option. Living in a temporal world where everything will be destroyed makes this decision easy, but it has been a battle. God has helped me stick with Him, and it is more amazing all the time.

Jesus disciples came to that same conclusion early in their relationship with Jesus. Jesus had just made a statement that most of the people listening did not understand because they did not understand why Jesus had come to earth. He made the statement that He was the living bread that came down from heaven and anyone who eats this bread will live forever. The Jews got angry, saying how can He give us His flesh to eat. Then Jesus said, "you cannot have life in you unless you eat the flesh of the Son of Man and drink His blood. He who feeds on My flesh and drinks My blood has (possesses now) eternal life. And I will raise him up [from the dead] on the last day. He who feeds on My flesh and drinks My blood dwells continually in Me, and I [in like manner dwell continually] in him." Jesus was describing how He wants to dwell in us and for us to dwell in Him. But the people hearing this missed what Jesus wanted. Like many today, they did not understand His heart and His desire to be one with them. Jesus' disciples sort of freaked out and said "this is a difficult, strange, and offensive statement; who can stand to hear it. "Many of his disciples left. Jesus looked at the twelve and said, "are you going also." Peter spoke up and said, "Lord, to whom shall we go? You have the words of eternal life." The disciples did not understand Jesus and what He was saying, but they knew He was the only one who had eternal life, so they had no where else to go. Jesus was the only one. Later on, they began to understand what He was talking about. He was talking about how close He wanted to be with them. It would be good to read this encounter (John 6:48-69).

I ended up using my architectural skills to make a living, helping people design the houses they dreamed of. But Jesus was number one; He was the only one with eternal life, and my career was not my answer to low self-esteem. My worth came from how God felt about me. He created me, and He has the right to define me. People can't define who I am. I found eternal love and eternal peace in Jesus. He loves me as much as the Father loves Jesus.

In Luke 10:38-42 NLT there is a very important encounter with Jesus where Jesus states this amazing potential we have with Him. It is illustrated in an encounter with Jesus that happened at Martha's house.

> *"As Jesus and the disciples continued on their way to Jerusalem, they came to a certain village where a woman named Martha welcomed him into her home.*
>
> *"Her sister, Mary, sat at the Lord's feet, listening to what he taught.*
>
> *"But Martha was distracted by the big dinner she was preparing. She came to Jesus and said, 'Lord, doesn't it seem unfair to you that my sister just sits here while I do all the work? Tell her to come and help me.'*
>
> *"But the Lord said to her, 'My dear Martha, you are worried and upset over all these details!*
>
> *"'There is only one thing worth being concerned about. Mary has discovered it* (or chosen it), *and it will not be taken away from her.'"*

This is profound. Jesus is saying, because He is eternal, "There is really only one thing <u>worth</u> being concerned about." That is an amazing statement, an all-consuming statement – a statement so powerful, so direct, that it swallows up everything in its path. Jesus said Mary had discovered the one thing <u>worth</u> being concerned about.

The one thing with unlimited potential is an eternal relationship with God. God is really the only thing in life that makes sense. Yes, we have to eat, provide shelter, but all these things will come to an end. A relationship with Jesus is the only thing that will last. He has the words of eternal life.

Remember, it's about potential or worth. This is what we are pursuing — eternal potential, eternal worth. Mary discovered that sitting at the feet of Jesus, looking Him in the eyes, and hearing what He was teaching was the one thing worth being ultimately concerned about.

This needs to be our one thing that everything else revolves around. We will have many worries come and go, but this is the center that all else revolves around. This we do not compromise on. This one-on-one connection with Jesus is the most important activity in our life. We may need to drop things that encroach on this and rearrange our schedules around this. It must never be crowded out by worthless things.

This is the nuclear bomb in our lives. It must be developed at all costs.

WHAT HAVE WE LEARNED FROM THIS CHAPTER?

1. Potential is having the capacity to become or develop into something in the future.

2. Everything we do has potential. Some things we do have little potential, some greater potential. Some things have destructive potential.

3. Things in the natural world have limited potential because everything is dying in the future. You, me, animals, plants, even our sun is dying and our planet and ultimately our universe.

4. Eternal things have much greater potential than temporal things.

5. Becoming one with Christ has the greatest potential of all, because He is eternal and the Creator of all things.

6. We can now have God living on the inside of us, the eternal God living inside of us. That is amazing!

7. Jesus' encounter with Mary and Martha in Luke 10:38-42 says it all.

PRAYER

God, reveal Yourself to me so that I may run after You. You are the only One worth pursuing, worth giving my all to. The potential You have given to me is staggering. God, don't let me crowd You out with worthless things, things that have little or no potential. Come, reveal Yourself to me. My heart tells me You are the pearl of great price — the One worth selling all to obtain. Reveal these things to my heart.

In heaven, all creatures are loved by God totally, and they love Him totally. They are creatures of love. To love Him and be loved by Him is the purpose of creation —
the purpose of life.

CHAPTER 22

GOD IS THE CENTER

The difference in the kingdom of earth and the kingdom of heaven is that in heaven Jesus, God the Father, and the Holy Spirit are the center, the focus. Everything revolves around them. They radiate love and life. God is the Creator, the Father who loves the children He created. He is the center because He is beyond incredible.

In heaven, all creatures are loved by God totally, and they love Him totally. They are creatures of love. To love Him and be loved by Him is the purpose of creation. This is what makes heaven, heaven. It is the type of relationship the beings in heaven have with the Creator. This is what makes heaven, heaven. So heaven is about a deep love relationship with God.

When we pray, "Thy will be done on earth, or in my heart, as it is in heaven," we are asking Christ to be the center of our affection; to love Him and be loved by Him; letting everything we do in this life rotate around this love relationship with the Father, Son, and the Holy Spirit. I arrange my life around them.

Like the planets orbiting the sun, our earth is in an orbit around the sun called the Goldilocks Zone, the perfect zone. The earth receives life from the sun. Without being close to the sun, all life on earth would die. All energy and life are generated by the sun, so the earth must stay close to the sun and not stray from its orbit, because the sun is the source.

So it is with our relationship with God. He is the Source of spiritual life. Apart from Him, we would die, so we stay close. We change our priorities, rearrange our schedules, pick and choose what we do based on Him being the center. I may add things to my life and get rid of things in my life, but these decisions are based on Him as the center and my life orbiting around Him.

When Jesus was here on earth, the Father was the center of His world. Everything Jesus did was because the Father was the center. Everything He did was from a deep love relationship with the Father. They loved each other eternally. It was a love deeper than anything we could imagine. They wanted nothing more than to be together.

When the crowds would descend on Jesus, He would leave and go to a lonely spot to commune with the Father. Nothing else mattered more to Him than deep fellowship with the Father. This frustrated the disciples because they could not figure out what motivated Jesus. Crowds would motivate most of us, but not Jesus. Fame would motivate a lot of us, but not

Jesus. Money did not motivate Jesus. Comforts in life did not motivate Jesus, nor the praise of men or disapproval of men.

Jesus said that He and the Father were one. This was His passion. This is what motivated Jesus, motivated Him to pray, motivated Him to spend all night with His Father, motivated Him to heal, to love, to go to the cross.

The life Jesus lived was a divine miracle. He was empowered by the Holy Spirit. For us to live a God-centered life, it will also be a divine miracle. In ourself, we do not have the key ingredients. Jesus said, *"Apart from Me ...you can do nothing"* (John 15:5). This is a freeing statement. It takes the focus off what we can do and puts the focus on what God can do. What is impossible with man is possible with God.

The heavenly lifestyle is a miracle from heaven. It's the Holy Spirit from heaven. Like the sun is to the earth, He gives us divine power and makes it possible.

So as Jesus taught us, the first thing we are to pray for is, "Your kingdom come into my life just like it is in heaven." Remember, you can't do it; it is a miracle that we pray for, and we become thankful for the small steps we take toward God and realize it is His power working in us that makes it possible.

In Matthew 6:31-34 NIV, Jesus lets us see what a life of making Him the center would look like:

"So do not worry, saying, 'What shall we eat?' or 'What shall we drink?' or 'What shall we wear?'

"For the pagans run after all these things, and your heavenly Father knows that you need them.

"But seek first his kingdom and his righteousness, and all these things will be given to you as well.

"Therefore do not worry about tomorrow, for tomorrow will worry about itself. Each day has enough trouble of its own."

God will give you all you need from day to day if you live for Him and make the kingdom of God your primary concern. Matthew 6:33.

WHAT HAVE WE LEARNED FROM THIS CHAPTER?

1. In heaven, God is the loving center. He radiates love and life to all beings.

2. What makes heaven, heaven is the relationship the beings in heaven have with the Creator. The creatures in heaven love God totally, and He loves them totally.

3. To love God and be loved by Him is the purpose of creation, the purpose of life.

4. God is the Source of divine life, like the sun is the source of all life on earth.

5. Like the Son, we must stay close to God and let our lives rotate around Him, because He is the Source of spiritual life.

6. In Matthew 6:31-34, Jesus sums up what a life of God being the center looks like.

PRAYER

Your desire is to be with me. Your heart wants me to be close to Your heart, and I want my life to orbit around Your love. Your love is better than life. It is more powerful than anything physical. It is the creative power of heaven. Your love created everything. Lord, pour Your love into my heart. It is the sunshine of heaven that allows me to grow into You. God, I want the purpose of my life to be Your purpose.

GOD IS IN LOVE WITH US ON A
SCALE WE CAN'T COMPREHEND.
HIS HIGHEST GOAL IS NOT OUR
HAPPINESS OR OUR PROSPERITY.
HIS HIGHEST GOAL
IS OUR COMPANIONSHIP.

CHAPTER 23

ONE THING IS ESSENTIAL

In this chapter, let's explore Jesus' encounter with Mary and Martha. We have touched on this in other chapters. I want to go a little deeper into this encounter, because I think this encounter may define the very kingdom of God.

Luke 10:38-42 of the *Message Bible* states:

"As they continued their travel, Jesus entered a village. A woman by the name of Martha welcomed him and made him feel quite at home. She had a sister, Mary, who sat before the Master, hanging on every word he said. But Martha was pulled away by all she had to do in the kitchen. Later, she stepped in, interrupting them. 'Master, don't you care that my sister has abandoned the kitchen to me? Tell her to lend me a hand.'

"The Master said, 'Martha, dear Martha, you're fussing far too much and getting yourself worked up over nothing.

One thing only is essential, and Mary has chosen it — it's the main course, and won't be taken from her."

What Jesus said here has staggering implications. Here, Jesus is uncompromisingly absolute. We all identify with Martha. She had a great heart. She was working so hard, but she was missing out on something amazing. Mary was sitting at the feet of Jesus, listening to Him speak, looking into His eyes, giving Him her total attention. Martha tries to pull Mary away from Jesus and get her busy. She pleads with Jesus to make Mary get up and help.

What Jesus said next has huge implications for us. He said, *"One thing only is essential, and Mary has chosen it."* I hope we can feel the impact of this statement. This statement sets the tone for the kingdom of God. We cannot let this statement slip by. We must look at it deeply and straight on. This statement is defining the kingdom of God. This statement is the number one desire of Jesus, His greatest desire, His passion, His purpose for us.

In the *Message Translation,* the word "essential" is used. Jesus said, *"One thing only is essential...."* The definition of "essential" is belonging to the very nature of a thing and therefore being incapable of removal without destroying the thing itself. What Jesus was saying is that sitting at His feet, listening to His voice, giving Him our undivided attention, loving Him with all our hearts, worshiping Him, being devoted to Him, allowing Him to be at home in us, live in us is essential. If we remove this or put it down on our priority list, we have removed the essential part of God's kingdom, and we have destroyed the thing itself. Oh, God, help us see that this is the very core of Your kingdom.

This is what is going on in heaven. They are gathered around the throne of God, drinking from His well, giving Him their whole attention, listening to His voice, loving Him with all their hearts, all their souls, all their minds, and strength. They are prostrate before Him. They can't pull themselves away from Him.

Revelation, chapters 4 and 5, indicate that this is the essential part of heaven; to separate from this would destroy the very nature of heaven. This is what makes heaven, heaven. When we pray, *"Thy kingdom come on earth as it is in heaven,"* this is what we are praying for.

When Martha tried to pull Mary away from Jesus because she had so much to do, Jesus said, *"Mary has chosen the better portion, and it won't be taken from her."* Other translations state it this way. The *Moffatt Translation* states, *"And she is not to be dragged away from it."* The *Phillips Translation* states, *"And you must not tear it away from her."* The *Weymouth Translation* states, *"And she shall not be deprived of it."*

These versions speak loudly to us. We must not let anything drag us away from the devotion Mary displayed. This is our destiny. In our busy world, many times this is what happens. We are dragged away by our own desires or pleasing others, etc. This one thing must be nonnegotiable. This is God's desire for us.

God is in love with us on a scale we can't comprehend. His ultimate goal is not our happiness or our prosperity. His ultimate goal is our companionship. We are married to Jesus. We are His bride. The one thing my wife desires is for me to stop my business, look her in the eyes, listen to her voice, and tell her I love her more than anyone.

It is no different with Jesus. We are in a marriage. "There is only one thing that is essential," so beautiful, so simple. We will have our struggles with giving Him our whole heart, giving Him our attention, sitting at His feet, and looking into His eyes. This may be the main struggle of your life. But God will help us. We just need to be persistent, ask for His help, and God will do the rest. This is the battle we must win!

WHAT HAVE WE LEARNED FROM THIS CHAPTER?

1. Many times Jesus taught through interactions with people. Some of His most profound lessons were encounters with people: the woman at the well, the woman caught in adultery; there are too many to name, but these were His greatest teachings.

2. Jesus' encounter with Mary and Martha was one of the most important encounters in the life of Jesus on earth. This encounter directs us to the core of the Gospel. It sums up what God's encounters with man are all about.

3. When Jesus entered the house of Mary and Martha, Mary was drawn to Jesus. She sat at His feet and was captivated by Him. She hung on to every word Jesus said. When Martha tried to drag her away, Jesus very

kindly made one of the most powerful statements in all of Scripture. He said, *"Martha, there is only one thing essential."* This is a most powerful statement. If you have a hundred things on a table, it looks so cluttered, and someone says, "There is only one thing here that is essential," part of you would say, "I want to keep all these things," and part of you would say, "Get rid of all the clutter; it is killing me. I want to simplify. I want to get down to what is essential." This is what Jesus just did. There is only one thing that is necessary. Let's declutter. To me that sounds so peaceful. The *only* thing that is essential in the kingdom of God is a deep personal relationship with Jesus.

4. God is in love with us on a scale we can't comprehend. His one goal is to be one with us, a oneness based on great love. Us in Him and Him in us. This is so marvelous. It's not religion, not just Bible reading, or church services. This is being united to God in a way unimaginable. Being united to God is the kingdom of God.

PRAYER

Oh God, awaken my heart to Your voice. Unite me with You where we become one. Pour Your love into my heart. I want to be in love with You, totally devoted to You. Help me to love You back the way You love me.

Note: Physical things can never satisfy the inner heart. This inner chamber is built for God. It is a sanctuary built for God. Only God can fill it and bring peace and fulfillment. There is nothing in this physical world that can satisfy that God-shaped space in our hearts; only God can fill it. This is why there is so much frustration, depression, strife, and discontentment in our world. This world was never designed to operate apart from God.

A. W. Tozer in his book, *The Pursuit of God,* talks about the age of religious complexity:

"Every age has its own characteristics. Right now we are in an age of religious complexity. The simplicity which is in Christ is rarely found among us. In its stead are programs, methods, organizations, and a world of nervous activities which occupy time and attention but can never satisfy the longing of the heart. The shallowness of our inner experience, the hollowness of our worship, and that servile imitation of the world which marks our promotional methods all testify that we, in this day, know God only imperfectly, and the peace of God scarcely at all.

"If we would find God amid all the religious externals, we must first determine to find Him, and then proceed in the way of simplicity. Now, as always, God discovers Himself to 'babes' and hides Himself in thick darkness from the wise and the prudent. We must simplify our approach to Him. We must strip down to essentials (and they will be found to be blessedly few). We must put away all effort to impress, and come with the guileless candor of childhood. If we do this, without doubt God will quickly respond.

"When religion has said its last word, there is little that we need other than God Himself. The evil habit of seeking *God-and* effectively prevents us from finding God in full revelation. In the *and* lies our great woe. If we omit the *and,* we shall soon find God, and in Him we shall find that for which we have all our lives been secretly longing.

"We need not fear that in seeking God only we may narrow our lives or restrict the motions of our expanding hearts. The opposite is true. We can well afford to make God our All, to concentrate, to sacrifice the many for the One."[3]

[3] A. W. Tozer. *The Pursuit of God,* Christian Publications, Inc., Camp Hill, Pennsylvania, © 1982, 1993, 17-18. All rights reserved. Printed in the United States of America.

SPENDING TIME WITH JESUS IS JOY
FOR HIM AND JOY FOR ME.
WE DELIGHT IN BEING TOGETHER.
HIS DESIRE IS FOR ME.

CHAPTER **24**

HOW WRITING THIS BOOK CHANGED MY LIFE

This book is the result of getting quiet and spending time with Christ as I said earlier. It was because of the Covid lockdown. I think many people's lives were changed during this lockdown.

God began to talk to me because I began to give Him my time and attention. Just like Mary of Bethany, I stopped my busy life and began to look into His eyes and listen to His voice (Luke 10:38-42). What I heard is what I recorded in this book.

There were several truths in this book that deeply impacted me. The first truth was how much and how extreme God's love is for me. Love is God's only motive toward me, and it is massive. This love He has for me means He wants to be very close to me because love wants to be close to the one it loves. That is the nature of love.

Jesus prayed in John 17:24, *"Father, I desire that they also whom You have entrusted to Me [as Your love gift to Me] may be with Me where I am...."* This prayer of Jesus greatly impacted me. In this prayer, Jesus wants me to be with Him – very close to Him. This was His greatest desire for me.

Another truth in this prayer is in the *Amplified Bible*: I am a love gift, given to Jesus from the Father. The reality that I am a love gift to Jesus changed how I view myself. Because of this, I began to spend time with Jesus. Realizing I am a love gift to Him from the Father, I could feel His pleasure when I would stop my busy life and talk with Him.

Jesus loves for me to be with Him because I am a love gift to Him. He lights up when I come to Him. So now, spending time with Jesus is joy for Him and joy for me. We delight in being together. His desire is for me.

Another truth that impacted me was that I can come to the very throne room of heaven and spend time with Him there. He is excited when I enter the throne room of heaven, the center of the universe. Jesus' death on the cross made this available to me. That is mind-blowing that I can go to the center of the universe and converse with God – the God who made billions of galaxies with billions of stars in each galaxy.

Another truth that affected me was that everything I see, taste, touch, and feel is temporal; everything around me is dying. So material things in this realm can never satisfy my heart because they are decaying. Therefore, I need to put my attention on eternal things that will ultimately satisfy and will not decay.

Everything I see, taste, touch, and feel will ultimately let me down. All I have acquired in my life will be taken from me at the moment of death. I think chapter 23 of this book affected me the most.

One thing is essential. When Jesus went to Mary and Martha's house in Bethany, Jesus made a statement that is so profound it is staggering. We talked about this encounter several times in the book. This statement greatly impacted me. Jesus said, *"Martha, dear Martha, you're fussing far too much and getting yourself worked up over nothing. One thing only is essential, and Mary has chosen it – it's the main course, and won't be taken from her"* (Luke 10:41-42 MSG).

That word "essential" impacted me. This one word was telling me that there was one thing that is essential, and everything else was not essential. This word means if you remove this one thing that is essential, you are destroying the entire system. So spending time with Jesus, like Mary, is the one essential thing in my life. If I remove this, I have destroyed God's purpose for my life.

As a result of these words from Jesus, I have made Him priority in my life. No matter how busy my day becomes, sitting at His feet, looking Him in the eyes, and letting Him talk to me is the one essential thing in my life. Even if it is only a short time, it is the most important thing I can do each day. Everything else must wait.

There were other things in this book that affected me. The Lord's Prayer tells us the first thing we are to pray for is His kingdom to come into our hearts like it is in heaven. My Christian life should look like heaven. The worship, the adoration, the love for Jesus that is in heaven is now my pattern. Heaven is the pattern. When I spend time with Jesus, I realize I have entered the heavenly realm; and what is going on around me is what is going on in heaven.

Another thing that affected me deeply was the absolute necessity of the Holy Spirit (chapter 11). Without the Holy Spirit, I can't even see the kingdom of God, so I have been asking on a daily basis for the Holy Spirit to help me see His beautiful kingdom. As I pray for the manifest presence of the Holy Spirit, I feel Him come. I feel His presence, and I am given the ability to fellowship with the Trinity on a deeper level. This is a prayer God loves to answer.

This verse has given me the confidence to pray for the conscious power of His Spirit to come. *"So if you sinful people know how to give good gifts to your children, how much more will your heavenly Father give the Holy Spirit to those who ask Him"* (Luke 11:13 NLT).

These are some of the things from this book that have changed my life permanently. Thank you for reading this book. These truths are what I fight for every day.

Don't take these things as rules, but as a love encounter with God. The things that have impacted me are not rules, but a pathway to a love relationship with God.

God is my safe place; as I spend time with Him, I am loved, cared for, and protected. I can tell Him anything, and He is not shocked, but listens and talks with me and loves me. It is this love that heals my heart.

Thank you so much for reading this book.

ABOUT THE AUTHOR

Allen grew up as an atheist. His love for science led him to the conclusion that science knew everything and had proven that there was no God.

When Allen was twenty-one, he started dating a girl who later became his wife. Her father was a very devout and godly man. He was not upset that his daughter was dating an atheist, for God had shown him in a dream that Allen was the man she would marry and not to worry. He just began to pray.

Allen began to feel a strange sensation, a feeling he had never felt before. This strange force was making him think about Jesus. He was puzzled and mystified by this strange force. He started to go to a church with her family. It wasn't long until that strange sensation led him to go forward in a church service and invite Jesus to come into his heart.

To his utter astonishment, Jesus came inside of him and he felt it. This encounter led Allen into the realm where God was real – a realm beyond this realm, the realm that created this realm. Allen spent several years in puzzling awe, trying to figure it all out. He thought it would not last because he had so many problems, but it did last because it was Jesus Christ who had entered him. As Allen found out, Jesus loved him so much, and Jesus would help him lovingly and gently get through all his troubles.

After studying architecture for five years, Allen transferred to Asbury University to study philosophy. Then something absolutely amazing happened. That same presence that had entered Allen descended on the whole university, and every student was deeply affected. It happened in a regular chapel service. It was so powerful that the chapel service lasted 185 hours, day and night. There are documentaries on YouTube describing the Asbury Revival.

After this experience, Allen wanted everyone to know about the real Jesus. He started a college ministry at the University of Kentucky where they held concerts with a thousand students attending. All of this happened during the Jesus Movement during the 1970's.

It was during the Jesus Movement that he saw hundreds of students ask Jesus to come on the inside of them. Allen never moved away from "youth ministry." Right before the Covid virus shut things down, Allen was working in public schools starting clubs and discipling teens and young adults.

When the school ministries shut down because of Covid, Allen decided to spend more time with Jesus. He wanted a deeper relationship and began to spend quality time with Christ. Jesus began to speak to him because he was now giving Jesus his time and attention. This book is the result of the time Allen spent talking and listening to Jesus.

Allen has an Associate Degree in Architecture and a B.A. Degree in Philosophy. He is married to Ruth, the girl he met when it all started. He has two sons and seven grandchildren. He lives in Tulsa, Oklahoma.

If you would like to contact Allen
he may be reached by email at:

allenmather1@gmail.com

Made in the USA
Middletown, DE
22 July 2023

35567725R00117